SOLO

SIGNE JOHANSEN

SOLO

the joy of cooking
for one

SIGNE JOHANSEN

bluebird
books for life

Contents

———

Introduction

Hi there,

Are you going solo in the kitchen for the first time? Congratulations, because cooking for one is a source of real joy! What a chance to be creative, to explore new ingredients and to practise dishes without the bother of worrying whether people will like what you make. You, my friend, are in for a treat.

I'll let you in on a secret every cook – whether she's solo or not – knows but rarely admits to: cooking for a crowd may sound fun in principle but in practise it's often a chore. Thanks to the weird world of performative cooking shows, we tend to think of cooking for others as a dazzling culinary cabaret. How exhausting that can be, even for the experienced cook. If you have fussy family members or housemates, you may even regard mealtimes with dread. The solo cook, however, can be gloriously selfish. Some ingrate doesn't like aubergine? Who cares! You want to add an extra clove or three of garlic but that annoying allium-phobe always kicks up a fuss? So what. You want to make something on toast but a snob-in-residence doesn't consider 'things on toast' a proper meal? Oh please do bore off.

You are in charge, you can do whatever you want, and by gosh please do tweak

the ingredients to your taste while using the recipes in this book. Nothing would make me more proud than knowing you have scribbled your adjustments in the margins: evidence of a clear commitment to use them again.

'Why bother cooking for myself when I can just grab a ready meal or a take-away?' you might ask, and that's a fair question. Sometimes the path of least resistance is irresistible. Once upon a time, I might have piously suggested that cooking a meal from scratch is always preferable, but what I would say now is just do what you have to do. Compromise is not a dirty word. We all take shortcuts sometimes. If nothing else, having a mediocre ready meal or expensive takeaway may spur you on to cooking that next meal from scratch.

With nearly three decades of cooking experience under my belt, I still maintain that when you need decompressing, time in the kitchen is time well-spent. Much like an afternoon nap, cooking solo can be immensely restorative. There is something both liberating and grounding about cooking for yourself. It's an affirmation of your self-worth and a welcome respite from life's many other challenges.

If you are a full-time solo cook, please consider this book a sisterly companion to get you going. I'd suggest starting by making a weekly meal plan and then source your ingredients accordingly. Intersperse a few simple meals with treats to look forward to during the week so you don't end up eating similar dishes day in and day out. Once you get in the habit, start mining other cookbooks for ideas, recipes that scale down to feed one or two (leftovers are never to be scoffed at), and take the time to savour both the planning and the actual cooking. Your confidence will increase as time goes on, and you'll learn to go with your gut: playing with ingredients from a fridge forage, say, or creating a cupboard casserole for one. The more you reframe your thinking that cooking for yourself is fun, the less you'll feel overwhelmed by the task itself.

As Nigel Slater once wrote, 'Cooking for yourself is simply a matter of self-respect' and this basic act of kindness towards yourself allows you to relax and experiment a little, and gives you the freedom to practise dishes without the fear of judgement from others. In Norwegian we say 'som plommen i egget': 'like the yolk in the egg' – i.e. what an ideal situation you're in when cooking solo. Now get planning!

A good cook stocks up

While resorting to a ready meal is hardly a moral failing, rare is the occasion when I've stood in a supermarket aisle and had a culinary epiphany: 'Why yes, tonight I shall cook a classic duck confit all for myself!' It's a fine idea in principle, but given that I can't remember half the ingredients and the cookbook is at home I'm usually stymied. Not to mention that the duck really needed to be slowly confit-ing itself since sometime around breakfast that day…

So if you're a novice cook, consider this my most useful advice to you: a good cook always has a well-stocked store-cupboard or larder (or whatever you want to call it). Why? It means you can grab ingredients on the run – perhaps a source of protein and greens or herbs – and cook something simple using a handful of condiments, spices, pastes. In other words: the odds and sods you have already in the kitchen. It really pays to be prepared, but also to think like a chef who has to make the most of ingredients available: do the occasional inventory of what's in your kitchen and that way you'll waste less. See my suggestions for stocking up on store-cupboard goods and fresh supplies on pages 194–198.

The chapters in this book

I find life as a solo cook means adapting a few habits. Instead of starting the day with toast, I'll often save bread for dishes you'll find in the Light Bites chapter. That simple shift in behaviour gives you more options later in the day. And believe me, the Croque Madame (page 18) is a supper fit for a queen.

Some evenings all you want to do is 'Netflix and Solo' (no, that is not a euphemism) or, indeed, shove your face in a pan of spaghetti while watching the *Barefoot Contessa*. Easy Weeknight Suppers is the chapter to hit when you want to treat yourself at the end of a busy day. The recipes here are my all-time favourites during the working week: dishes that zing with flavour and fresh, vibrant colours. Just because you're cooking solo doesn't mean you're not eating as much with your eyes as the other senses. And yes, it's perfectly acceptable to eat spaghetti straight from the pan. It should be noted that all these recipes can easily be scaled up to feed two people, so you can 'Netflix and Duo', as it were.

In my previous book, *How to Hygge*, I wrote about how often we needlessly overcomplicate our lives. If you're in a lather of indecision about what to eat I find the easiest solution is to opt for a dish that has a handful of ingredients. Sometimes the last thing our wired brains need is a long list of things to buy for one particular dish, and a complex, time-consuming method to contend with. One-pan Wonders is the chapter to turn to for this particular moment. Less mess, less washing up, less faff all round.

As I've already mentioned, keeping a well-stocked kitchen gives you flexibility. If you have the inclination, making a few dishes in advance is a smart move that can optimise your time, so I've included a Make Ahead chapter. Not only do you save the odd half hour later in the week when you might be swamped with work, or feeling low thanks to a seasonal bout of the sniffles, but you know exactly what goes into each dish. Of course, takeaways and ready meals are useful standbys, but a little forward planning definitely reaps rewards. As keen cooks will tell you,

there's something indefinably satisfying about making a dish in advance: you'll feel super-smug knowing that it's waiting for you at home.

Swedish statistician Hans Rosling once said, 'Let the world surprise you', and this is essentially my philosophy of cooking and eating. I'll try anything once. Although I love the flavours and ingredients of my native Scandinavia, there is much delight to be found in food from the Middle East, Europe, Japan, Korea, India, Latin America... While I have yet to experience the culture and try the food of other parts of the world, staying curious about different cultures and their dishes is essential to staving off any looming apathy or boredom that might set in when repeatedly cooking with the same ingredients. The dishes in Salads, Mezze and Tapas transport me to places of heady, enticing flavours, and require an economy of effort but bring so much contentment.

The Simple Pleasures chapter is really one to turn to at any time of the day. Dishes on these pages aren't always complete meals, but ones I turn to when I'm feeling snacky, or indeed a little crabby. Rather than diving into a box of biscuits or a bag of crisps, these recipes are a comforting balm on trying days. For days when you're out and about, treats like the dates with tahini (page 146) are a great portable snack – perhaps for a work-break nibble or a solo picnic – and the chilled soba noodles (page 134) make an ideal packed lunch.

We live in an age during which meditation and 'mindfulness' are all the rage, and whilst many roll their eyes at the notion of 'self-care', I've learnt that time spent cooking something simple in the kitchen – and it can be pretty much any kitchen – is both meditative and deeply restorative. My Lazy Weekends chapter is included with this in mind. Some cooks talk about the state of 'flow' they feel when they're making a dish. It's a way for your brain to switch off from all the noise outside. Try channelling a little of that next time you're in the kitchen on the weekend, you'll be surprised at how calming it can be.

There was some discussion about whether to include Sweet Things in this book. Supermarkets report that their solo bestsellers are desserts, so why would anyone go to the trouble of making one for themselves? Although I'm partial to the occasional bought

pudding, I've long been a fan of home-baking and rustling up easy puddings. Given that we live in an age that is wary of too much sugar, you'll find the sweetness of these recipes is muted compared to commercial desserts, but no less delicious for it. I've included muffins and cookies which you can share with friends, colleagues and family – after all, just because you're cooking solo doesn't mean you're a hermit. I'm delighted this chapter made the cut and I hope you'll give a few of the recipes a try next time your sweet tooth craves a homemade treat.

All that remains for me to say is: you've got this! Now go have a good time in the kitchen.

Sig x

It should be noted that since being asked to write this book, I got engaged and married, and while there have been plenty of moments during married life when I've still cooked for myself alone, these recipes scale up easily to feed a duo, even a trio.

Light Bites and Things on Toast

Croque Madame

This Croque Madame eschews a traditional béchamel sauce topping for the simple reason that, given the choice between taking time to cook delicious, creamy spinach and a boring, bland sauce, spinach wins every time. I've cheated by using crème fraîche, but you can leave it out and add a little mustard and nutmeg to the cheese as a final flourish before grilling.

butter, for frying
2 slices of sourdough bread,
  country loaf or spelt bread,
  one slice lightly buttered on
  one side
handful of grated cheese –
  a mix of Gruyere, Parmesan
  and mozzarella (or use
  whatever you have/like)
1 tsp crème fraîche
½ tsp Dijon or English mustard
1 egg

For the creamy spinach
100g baby spinach, washed
1 tsp butter
1 small garlic clove, finely
  chopped
2 tsp crème fraîche
nutmeg, to taste
sea salt and freshly ground
  black pepper

Start by making the creamy spinach. Put the spinach leaves in a small saucepan to wilt over a low heat, then place in a sieve and drain away all the excess liquid, pressing it with a spoon. Heat the butter in the same saucepan over a medium heat until foaming, then add the garlic and cook for 30 seconds, or until it becomes translucent and turns lightly golden. Stir in the crème fraîche, then season with a grating or two of nutmeg. Fold in the drained spinach, season with salt and pepper and set aside.

Melt 2 teaspoons of butter in a frying pan or skillet over a high heat until foaming. Add the unbuttered slice of bread to the pan and smear the creamy spinach over it, then add about half of the grated cheese. Top with the buttered slice of bread (butter-side up), then, when the first slice is golden brown and crisp on the bottom, turn the whole thing over carefully and repeat the frying on the other side. Preheat the grill to medium, place the Croque Madame on a baking sheet or in a roasting dish, top with more cheese, the crème fraîche and mustard and grill until bubbling and slightly caramelised. Fry the egg in some butter in a small skillet or frying pan, place it on the Croque Madame and eat immediately.

Variation: Add a slice of good-quality ham or smoked salmon with the spinach for extra flavour and protein.

Ricotta, fig, pomegranate molasses, toasted almond, mint and sea salt

Here's a delicious open sandwich or *tartine* to start the day, or to rustle up if you're feeling snacky – the gentle ricotta flavour is given a lift with figs and mouth-puckering pomegranate molasses.

---

1 slice of bread of choice (or a few pieces of crispbread)
2 heaped tbsp ricotta
1 large ripe fig, thinly sliced (you can also use dried fig)
sprinkle of toasted flaked almonds
1 tsp pomegranate molasses
leaves from 1 sprig of mint
sea salt

Toast your bread, then spread the ricotta on top. Follow with the sliced fig and flaked almonds and drizzle with the pomegranate molasses before adding the mint leaves and finally sprinkling it with a little sea salt.

Variations:
– Try this with plum, peach or nectarine, too (in place of the figs).
– To make this more savoury, top the ricotta with sliced radishes, grated carrot, grilled asparagus, par-boiled tenderstem or purple sprouting broccoli, broad beans, sliced cucumber or pickles.

Leftovers: Use the rest of your tub of ricotta to make the Lemon, Courgette and Ricotta Fritters (page 141) or the Ricotta and Parmesan Gnudi with Sage Brown Butter (pages 104–5). Alternatively, just add lemon zest and toss with freshly cooked pasta, some herbs and greens of choice for a light supper.

Cardamom-poached apricots with vanilla quark and pistachios on toast

These apricots are perfect for mornings when you've run out of jam. Apricots have the most gorgeous colour, but too often I find fresh ones taste quite bland, so this is one way of gently enhancing them. Cardamom is a much-used spice in my household – mostly in baking – and it works wonders on apricots, too. If you're fortunate enough to have a glut, scale up the quantities of fruit, cardamom and honey to make a batch of poached apricots and keep them covered in the fridge for up to a week. (Pictured on pages 22–3.)

2 fresh apricots, halved and stoned
2 green cardamom pods, lightly crushed or ½ tsp ground cardamom
1 tsp acacia honey, plus extra to serve (optional)
½ tsp vanilla extract
4 tbsp plain, full-fat quark
1 large slice of wholemeal, rye or sourdough bread
butter, for spreading (optional)
a few plain unsalted pistachios, crushed, or pistachio slivers

Put the apricots in a small saucepan, add the cardamom and honey and cover the apricots with water. Poach for 15–20 minutes over a low heat, or until they're soft and fragrant.

Meanwhile, thoroughly mix the vanilla and quark in a bowl. Toast the bread and spread it with butter (if using), then spread the quark on the toast once it has cooled slightly. Spoon the poached apricots over the quark and scatter with crushed pistachios or pistachio slivers. Add a drizzle of honey if you have a sweet tooth.

Variations:
– Use different spices such as cinnamon in the poaching liquor. Adding a star anise to the mix gives it a bracing aniseed flavour.
– Try adding a few cooling Earl Grey tea leaves to contrast with the warming spices.
– Use dried apricots, if you have some in the cupboard. I sometimes poach whatever dried fruit I have (apricots, prunes, figs, cranberries, pears and sour cherries are all ideal), increasing the poaching time if necessary, so they plump up. Use on toast, as a porridge topping or to give Greek yoghurt a bit of oomph.
– Substitute apricots for plums.
– Fromage frais or ricotta work really well instead of quark, as does Greek yoghurt.

Stichelton, vanilla and acacia honey-glazed walnuts, mint and pear

Here's a dish for those days when only a hefty hit of blue will satisfy a cheese craving. Stichelton, an unpasteurised version of Stilton made on the Welbeck Estate in Nottinghamshire by ace cheesemaker Joe Schneider, is available from Neal's Yard Dairy. It ranks as my favourite blue cheese in the world, alongside Irish Cashel Blue and gorgonzola. Actually, I just love blue cheese in general. If you can source it, I recommend trying this wonderful cheese, but of course a good-quality stilton will also be delicious. (Pictured on pages 22–3.)

1 slice of wholemeal bread
a decent amount of Stichelton
  (or blue cheese of choice)
1 small ripe pear, cored and
  thinly sliced (skin on)
1 tsp acacia honey (or other
  delicate honey)
¼ tsp vanilla extract (or the
  seeds from a tiny sliver of
  vanilla bean)
3 walnuts, crumbled
a few mint leaves

Toast the bread, then spread the Stichelton on top. Arrange half the pear slices over the cheese. Mix the honey and vanilla together, scatter the walnuts over the cheese and glaze them with the vanilla honey. Garnish with the mint leaves and serve with the remaining pear slices on the side.

Variations:
– The nuttiness of good wholemeal bread pairs well with this combination of ingredients but you can also use rye, spelt or a sourdough bread.
– Use thyme instead of mint to give the open sandwich a woody flavour.

Wild mushrooms on toast

When in season, wild mushrooms are a treat: full of rich, contrasting flavours that turn classic mushrooms on toast into something very special indeed. This open sandwich is so good on its own but needless to say, if you're after a little extra protein then top it with a fried egg. (Pictured on pages 22–3.)

2 slices of sourdough bread
or bread of choice
25g butter, plus extra to serve
(optional)
1 tbsp vegetable or sunflower
oil, plus extra to serve
(optional)
1 sprig of thyme
150g wild mushrooms, wiped
clean and roughly chopped
1 garlic clove, finely chopped
or thinly sliced
small bunch of flat-leaf
parsley, finely chopped
splash of lemon juice or vinegar
sea salt and freshly ground
black pepper

Toast the bread so the slices are nice and crisp.

Heat the butter and oil in a medium frying pan over a medium-high heat until the butter is foaming, then add the sprig of thyme (this flavours the fat), followed by the wild mushrooms. Season with salt and pepper, remove the thyme sprig, and cook until the mushrooms are golden brown and a little caramelised. Keep tossing them so they don't burn on the bottom of the pan.

Turn down the heat to low. Add the garlic and cook for a further minute, then add the parsley and a splash of lemon juice or vinegar to add a little vibrant acidity.

Drizzle a little oil on your pieces of toast or spread them with butter and top with the wild mushrooms. Eat immediately.

Variations:
– A little heat from chilli, cayenne or Tabasco wouldn't go amiss.
– Adding a tiny amount of Marmite to the pan gives depth of flavour to the mushrooms.
– Vary the herbs: rosemary, oregano and basil would all work instead of the thyme or parsley.

Anchovy, olive and almond tapenade

Tapenade is a classic example of what can come from a good fridge or store-cupboard forage: it requires an assortment of intensely-flavoured ingredients, simply blended together and consumed with rather more toast or melbas than you might anticipate. Store-bought versions are often too bitter for my taste, a likely result from using quite sharp olives. This version, however, is a savoury delight. Feel free to play with the proportions of ingredients: add more or fewer anchovies, or increase the mustard if you wish. A little chilli too, perhaps. As always, season to your taste.

1 small bunch of parsley leaves (or marjoram, oregano and basil), washed, plus extra to serve
5 green olives, preferably Nocellara or Spanish manzanilla olives, pitted
5 wrinkly black olives, pitted
5 unsalted roasted almonds
2 tinned or jarred anchovies (in oil)
1 garlic clove
1 tsp capers, rinsed
½ tsp wholegrain mustard
grated zest and juice of ½ unwaxed lemon
olive oil
sea salt and freshly ground black pepper

Place all the ingredients (except the oil and seasoning) in a blender or food processor and pulse for a few seconds, adding 2–3 tablespoons of olive oil after initial pulsing, then pulse again to bring it all together. If you like it really creamy, add more olive oil. If you like it quite chunky just pulse a few times until you have a rough paste. You can chop the herbs by hand and crush all the other ingredients together using a pestle and mortar instead, if you prefer.

Keep the tapenade in an airtight container in the fridge for up to a week. An extra spritz of lemon juice on the surface will slow down the oxidation process and keep the tapenade fresh for longer.

Pan con tomate

Some dishes never go out of style and although 'tomato bread' doesn't sound quite as redolent of Iberian sunshine and holidays as the original Spanish, this recipe is always a winner, no matter where you are. I love the version served at London's Barrafina restaurant and this is the Solo cook's recipe *para uno*.

Una receta muy fácil!

2.5cm-thick slice of fluffy, white country bread, sourdough or similar
½ small garlic clove, peeled and halved
2 ripe tomatoes of the season, such as cherry, plum or heritage, halved
1 tbsp regular or extra-virgin olive oil (if you like a peppery flavour, opt for the latter)
sea salt and freshly ground black pepper

Toast the bread until golden and crisp on the edges, then take the cut sides of the garlic and rub them vigorously all over the crusty bread while it's still warm.

Next, either scoop out the seeds and juice from the tomatoes using a spoon, or as Barrafina suggests, use your hands to force them on to the surface of the garlic toast. Make sure there's an even layer of tomato to cover the garlic, then drizzle with the olive oil and season with salt and pepper. Eat.

Variations:
– The beauty of this recipe is its simplicity, but you can add spices such as fresh red or green chilli, pimenton picante, a light dusting of cayenne (the emphasis being on 'light') or some smoky ancho chilli flakes over the tomato.
– Herbs are welcome if you have some parsley or coriander to use up.
– Make this into a more substantial dish by adding avocado, cheese or sardines.

Zingy smoked salmon and avocado tartare

There is an unspoken rule in the Johansen family: don't mess with the fish. We don't like a lot of embellishment when it comes to our prized Norwegian seafood. This isn't an exclusively Johansen quirk – across Scandinavia you'll find that seafood is treated with reverence. If it's fresh, let it shine.

So this tartare is something of a departure from the family tradition of serving smoked salmon simply with a wedge of lemon, some buttered toast and maybe a crack of black pepper. It's loosely inspired by the flavours of Mexico but I can't claim it's authentic (whatever that means) in any way so hence the name: a zingy tartare.

1 small ripe avocado or
  ½ large one, halved, stoned
  and flesh diced
grated zest and juice of
  1 unwaxed lime
1 spring onion, thinly sliced
1 green chilli, finely chopped
  (deseed it if you wish)
handful of coriander, leaves
  roughly chopped
green or red Tabasco, to taste
a few slices of smoked salmon,
  roughly chopped into small
  chunks
sea salt (optional)
as many tortilla chips or pita
  breads as you like, to serve

Mix the avocado with the lime zest and juice, spring onion, chilli and coriander leaves in a bowl and season to taste with Tabasco. If the smoked salmon is quite mild then add a little sea salt to the avocado mixture but if the salmon is salty, err on the side of caution.

Gently fold the smoked salmon into the avocado mixture and eat within an hour or so (the lime juice eventually 'cooks' the smoked salmon which alters its silky texture), scooping it up with the tortilla chips or pita.

Leftovers: If you're using half a large avocado, see the Crab, Avocado, Broad Bean and Grilled Gem Lettuce Salad (page 46) or the Savoury Cornmeal Pancakes with Avocado Salsa and Bacon (page 163).

Scandi shrimp on crispbread

This riff on Toast Skagen, a popular dish across seafaring Scandinavia, is a recipe I turn to whenever I get a little homesick for the cold, frozen North. It's traditionally made with mayonnaise but I'm not the biggest fan of mayo – Greek yoghurt makes for a fresher dish.

1 standard-size round Peter's Yard crispbread (or 2 and with a little less mixture spread across it)
butter, softened
2 tbsp full-fat Greek yoghurt
1 sprig of dill, chopped, plus extra to garnish
1 small shallot, thinly sliced and placed in a bowl of iced water for a few minutes, then drained
5cm piece of cucumber, chopped
grated zest and juice of ¼ unwaxed lemon (juice optional)
50g cooked and peeled North Sea shrimp
sea salt and freshly ground black pepper

Start by spreading the crispbread(s) with a decent layer of butter.

Mix the yoghurt in a bowl with the dill, drained shallot, cucumber and lemon zest. Taste and season with pepper (and a little salt, if you think it needs it).

Spread the yoghurt mixture over the crispbread and top with the shrimps, some extra dill and a spritz of lemon juice if you wish.

Spicy, garlicky, lemony, herby sardines on toast

Some people find the idea of tinned oily fish a little off-putting, as if a tin of sardines is no better than glorified cat food and should be avoided. With respect, I disagree. Sardines, mackerel and anchovies are essential staples in any decent cook's cupboard, and I've lost count of the times one of them has come to the rescue when I've been too tired to cook anything elaborate.

Buy the best tinned fish you can afford – supermarket own-brand ones are usually great, and for a treat the range from Spanish brand Ortiz is exceptional.

1 long slice of sourdough
   bread or 2 smaller slices of
   regular-sized bread
1 garlic clove, peeled and
   halved
olive oil or butter (optional)
1 x 80–85g tin of sardine
   piccanti (spicy sardines)
1 tsp fresh oregano leaves
1 sprig of parsley, leaves
   finely chopped
grated zest and juice of
   ½ unwaxed lemon
a few ripe tomatoes, sliced

Toast the bread until crispy and golden. Rub the cut sides of the garlic clove vigorously all over the crusty bread while it's still warm. I like to drizzle a little of the oil from the sardine tin over the bread but if you prefer, just use plain olive oil (or butter) instead.

Arrange the tomato slices over the bread, followed by the sardine fillets and herbs and squeeze the lemon juice on the herbs. Scatter with the lemon zest and eat while warm.

Variations:
– If you're ravenous with hunger then the flesh of a small, destoned avocado on the garlicky toast is a welcome addition.
– Add some leftover roasted lemony vegetables from page 72 to the sandwich if you wish.
– Other herbs to try include marjoram, chives, thyme, rosemary or basil, but basil can be a bit of a bully (depending on how robust a flavour the leaves have), so I prefer the oregano/parsley combo.

Easy
Weeknight
Suppers

—

Roasted sea bass with rosemary, lemon and garlic

I love roasting a whole fish with herbs, lemon and garlic – the smells wafting from the oven as all those flavours come together while the fish cooks make any takeaway seem desultory in comparison. You can use other white fish instead of the sea bass if you prefer, such as sea bream.

1 small sea bass (about 400g) –
  ask your fishmonger to gut
  and de-scale it for you
olive oil, for drizzling
1 unwaxed lemon, thinly sliced
3 garlic cloves, thinly sliced
leaves from 2 sprigs of rosemary
1 shallot, thinly sliced
sea salt and freshly ground
  black pepper

For the salad
1 baby gem lettuce, leaves
  separated, washed and dried
1 small carrot
1 shallot, finely chopped and
  placed in a bowl of iced water
  for a few minutes
wine or cider vinegar

Preheat the oven to 200°C/gas mark 6.

Cut three shallow diagonal slits into the skin on each side of the fish and carefully drizzle a little oil over the skin, gently rubbing it over the fish until it's completely coated in oil. Season the cavity of the fish with salt and pepper, then stuff it with most of the lemon, garlic and rosemary, along with the shallot, and finish with a little drizzle of olive oil to coat it all. Put the fish into a roasting tray.

Place a sliver of garlic and lemon and some rosemary in each of the diagonal slits. Sprinkle salt over the skin on both sides, then place the fish in the oven and bake it for 15–20 minutes. Check the fish is done by gently poking the flesh – it should look white and opaque. Don't let it stay in the oven for too long as the fish overcooks quickly.

While the fish cooks, make a little salad. Place the lettuce leaves in a small bowl and roughly grate the carrot on top, then garnish with the drained, chopped shallot. Drizzle oil and vinegar over the salad, to taste.

Remove the fish from the oven and eat while hot, with the salad.

Scandi hot-smoked trout with dill-buttered Jersey Royal potatoes and quick-pickled cucumber

We have a saying in our family that Scandinavian seafood is the healthiest 'fast food' in the world. A fridge containing pickled herrings, hot-smoked trout and Abba anchovies means we can rustle up simple, nutritious and delicious suppers in a matter of minutes.

Britain's Jersey Royals are always a treat when they come into season so I've included this dish as a spring or summer one but it can of course be made at any time of year, using a different sort of potato. You can make this dish using hot-smoked salmon, too.

5 Jersey Royal potatoes (or as many as you like)
juice of 1 unwaxed lemon (grate the zest into the crème fraîche if you wish, or keep the squeezed lemon halves for drinks)
1–2 tsp caster sugar (or according to taste)
½ cucumber, cut into ribbons with a vegetable peeler or thinly sliced
1 tbsp butter
a few sprigs of dill, finely chopped (reserve some to garnish if you like)
1–2 fillets of hot-smoked trout
1 heaped tbsp crème fraîche
sea salt and freshly ground black pepper

Bring a small saucepan to the boil with lightly salted water (a teaspoon of salt will suffice) and cook the Jersey Royals for 10–15 minutes until they're cooked through.

Meanwhile, make the quick cucumber pickle. Mix the lemon juice and sugar in a bowl. Taste it – I like it very sour. Add the cucumber ribbons or slices, toss and set aside.

When the potatoes are cooked, drain them and return them to the hot pan. Let them steam dry for a few minutes to get rid of excess moisture, then add the butter, dill and a good crack of black pepper, tossing the potatoes so they're evenly coated in the dill butter.

Place the hot-smoked trout fillets on a plate and add the dill-buttered potatoes. Lift the cucumber out of the lemon juice and place it near the fish (the lemon juice can be added to a glass of sparkling water for a refreshing drink to accompany the dish) and add the crème fraîche.

Eat immediately. A glass of really chilled Riesling goes well with the dish, or any white wine that you favour.

Frutti di mare al cartoccio

Enclosing in a parcel then baking it is a really easy way to cook seafood, and you can add a portion of pasta – cooked al dente – to the parcel if you want to make it an even more filling meal.

200g mix of frozen, raw fruits
  de mer, defrosted (or fresh,
  if you can source them)
5 cherry tomatoes, halved
1 small fresh green chilli,
  finely chopped
1 tinned anchovy (in oil),
  finely chopped
1–2 garlic cloves, finely
  chopped
1–2 sprigs of flat-leaf parsley,
  leaves roughly chopped, plus
  extra to serve
2 thin slices of unwaxed lemon
a splash of white or red wine,
  or vermouth/sherry (optional)
sea salt and freshly ground
  black pepper
slice of bread, to serve

Preheat the oven to 220°C/gas mark 7.

Put a 50cm-long sheet of aluminium foil on the work surface. Cut a piece of parchment the same size as the foil and place it on top. Fold the double layer in half to create a 4-layer square of parchment and foil. Bring the sides of the square up to create a vessel and crimp the edges to seal the layers together, leaving the opening until you have filled the parcel. Place it on a baking sheet or in a roasting dish.

Combine all the ingredients (except the seasoning and the bread) in a medium bowl, so the seafood mixes with the rest of the ingredients. Season with salt and pepper and mix again. If you have some wine, vermouth or sherry handy, add a splash to the bowl for extra acidity and depth of flavour. Scoop the mixture carefully into the parcel and seal the sides of the parcel together so it's airtight.

Cook in the oven for 15–18 minutes, or until the parcel has completely puffed up.

Remove from the oven, carefully open the parcel and sprinkle a little extra fresh parsley on top. Scoff the lot with a slice of bread to mop up all the juices.

Prawn, lime, peanut and herb rice noodles

This is a super dish to rustle up when you're tired and hungry – it takes just minutes to prepare and can be eaten either hot or at room temperature. An ice-cold beer alongside wouldn't go amiss, but a glass of green or jasmine tea also makes an excellent accompaniment.

100g thick or thin rice noodles
vegetable or sunflower oil,
  for frying
150g raw shelled prawns
  (or defrosted frozen ones)
1–2 garlic cloves, finely chopped
1 green chilli, finely chopped
1 spring onion, thinly sliced
small bunch of mint and/or
  coriander, roughly chopped
1 small carrot, coarsely grated
  or cut into ribbons with
  a vegetable peeler
small handful of salted peanuts,
  roughly crushed
sea salt and freshly ground
  black pepper
lime wedge, to serve (optional)

For the sauce
grated zest and juice of
  2 unwaxed limes
1 tbsp fish sauce
1 tbsp soft light brown sugar
  or palm sugar
1 red chilli, finely diced
1 garlic clove, finely grated

Combine the ingredients for the sauce in a bowl.

Cook the rice noodles according to the packet instructions until al dente, drain, toss them in the sauce and set aside.

Meanwhile, heat a little oil in a skillet or frying pan over a medium heat, add the prawns and fry for a few minutes until golden-pink and opaque – remove them from the pan as soon as they're done so they don't become tough. Add the garlic, chilli and spring onion to the same pan once you've removed the prawns and fry gently for a couple of minutes, then remove the pan from the heat and return the prawns to the pan so all the flavours blend.

Serve the noodles in a shallow pasta bowl or on a dinner plate and scatter over the prawns, herbs, carrot and crushed peanuts. Season to taste and add a lime wedge, if you wish.

Variation: Feel free to add other vegetables such as chopped pepper, broccoli or bean sprouts (raw or cooked). I sometimes like to add edamame beans, broad beans and grated courgette, too.

Crab, avocado, broad bean and grilled gem lettuce salad

I first had grilled lettuce with a roast chicken dish in Copenhagen and wondered why I had never cooked it this way before. Grilling the base ingredient of a salad may not be the most obvious move but the slight char and caramelisation you get from the lettuce really pairs well with crab.

Salad cream – or 'white ketchup' as it's known in our family – makes an appearance here, too. I know it's not fashionable, but the vinegar kick of salad cream complements the grilled lettuce so well. If the idea of using salad cream absolutely horrifies you, simply leave it out.

handful of broad beans
  (about 75g), podded
1 baby gem lettuce head,
  quartered lengthways
light olive or vegetable oil,
  for brushing
1 small ripe avocado, halved,
  stoned and flesh sliced
100–120g white and brown
  crab meat (1 portion)
⅓ cucumber, cut into ribbons
  with a vegetable peeler
1 fresh red chilli, finely chopped

To serve (optional)
Tabasco
salad cream, vinaigrette or
  mayonnaise
sea salt and freshly ground
  black pepper
1 small unwaxed lemon
Melba toasts or similar
  (optional)

Bring a saucepan of water to the boil, add the broad beans and cook for a few minutes, then drain and transfer to a bowl of iced water to cool, so they keep their vibrant colour. Drain and pop the beans out of their skins into a bowl.

Heat a skillet or frying pan over a medium heat or preheat the grill to medium. Lightly brush the lettuce quarters with oil then fry or grill for a minute on each side, until golden brown (if grilling, watch carefully to make sure they don't scorch).

Place the lettuce pieces on a plate or in a wide, shallow pasta bowl. Top with the avocado, broad beans and crab meat. Add the cucumber ribbons and scatter over the chopped red chilli.

Finishing the dish is a matter of personal taste: drizzle over a little Tabasco, salad cream or whatever condiment you fancy. Be judicious. You want the crab to be the star of the dish, and the condiment to coax all the flavours together. Season to taste (a spritz of lemon zest never goes amiss in a crabby salad). Serve with toast, if you like.

Note: Try 'white ketchup' instead of mayo in a tuna sandwich (and swap the traditional celery for German or Polish gherkins. Seriously, give it a try), or add it to a green herb dressing for potato salad.

Spiced chickpeas with tomatoes and spinach

Here is one of the most popular reader recipes from *The Ultimate Student Cookbook*, a book I worked on many years ago with a team assembled by my friend and mentor Fiona Beckett, and I still make it to this day. A staple for autumn and winter evenings when you need something really spicy and comforting to warm the soul.

2 tbsp vegetable oil
1 medium onion, finely chopped
2 garlic cloves, finely chopped
½ tsp ground cumin
½ tsp coriander seeds
a pinch of ground turmeric
a pinch of chilli powder
  or cayenne
3 large tomatoes, roughly
  chopped, or 1 x 400g tin of
  plum or chopped tomatoes
1 x 400g tin of chickpeas,
  drained and rinsed
splash of water/stock (optional)
2 large handfuls of fresh
  spinach, washed
1 tsp vinegar (optional)
a pinch of sugar (optional)
sea salt and freshly ground
  black pepper
wedge of lemon, to serve
1–2 spoonfuls of Greek yoghurt
  or labneh, to serve
pita bread or other flatbread,
  to serve (optional)

Heat the oil in a saucepan or a deep frying pan over a medium heat. Add the onion and cook for 4–10 minutes until translucent and soft (how long this will take depends on the heat and the onion – onions are fickle little bastards).

Add the garlic and spices and cook for a further minute or so until the garlic is translucent but not brown. Add the tomatoes and chickpeas and simmer for about 10 minutes, to allow the flavours to mingle and the mixture to thicken. If it looks dry, add a splash of water or stock. Season lightly.

Add the spinach. If the moisture from the spinach makes the sauce a little watery reduce the mixture again for a few minutes before seasoning. If you find the tomatoes have quite a 'tinny' flavour, add the vinegar and sugar to neutralise it.

Serve hot with a spritz of lemon juice, Greek yoghurt or labneh, and pita bread or flatbread.

Leftovers: Stuff the mixture into a wrap the next day, or add a cupful of stock and make it into a soup.

Variations:
– For an Iberian twist, substitute the spices for a generous pinch of pimenton or paprika.
– For a flavour of India, add a thimbleful of freshly grated ginger, a smidgeon of ground cardamom and garam masala or curry powder.

Succotash salad

A good salad is a joy during the spring and summer months, but there are times when I tire of green leaves as the base and elect to make an old-fashioned chopped salad. Succotash fits the bill perfectly. Essentially, it's a mix of corn and broad beans that you can embellish according to what's in season, or what's in your larder. You can scale it down by half for a single portion but it's so delicious I love having it again the next day.

200g frozen or fresh
  broad beans
1 x 190g tin of sweetcorn,
  drained (160g drained weight)
1 small red pepper, halved,
  deseeded and chopped to
  a similar size as the corn
  or beans
1 small shallot, finely chopped
  and soaked in iced water for a
  few minutes
1–2 tbsp sliced pickled jalapeño
  peppers (from a jar)
small bunch of basil
1 unwaxed lime
olive oil, to taste
sea salt and freshly ground
  black pepper

Cook the beans for a few minutes in boiling water (not long – they should just be al dente) then drain and cool in iced water. If you like to see the vivid green of the broad beans, spend a few minutes shelling them after cooking. It's no big deal if you can't be bothered.

In a medium salad bowl mix together the beans with the sweetcorn, red pepper, drained shallot and jalapeño peppers. Shred the basil leaves into the mixture and finely grate the lime zest in, then halve the lime and squeeze in the juice from both halves. If you like a really tart flavour, add more lime juice (or some lemon juice) as you see fit.

Drizzle a few tablespoons of olive oil over the lot and stir through. Season with salt and pepper.

Variations:
– Add grilled chicken or crispy fried bacon.
– Try adding salty cheese like feta, fried halloumi or pecorino for extra flavour.

Grilled harissa chicken with preserved lemon, barley couscous and herbs

We've all gone mad for harissa in recent years and it's no wonder: this potent, fiery paste with a flaming red colour has the ability to magically lift all kinds of dishes. I keep a jar in my fridge and a backup in the cupboard – that's how much I can't live without it. The best I've come across is Belazu's rose harissa, which is widely available in the UK.

2 tsp harissa paste
2 tsp vegetable or sunflower
  oil, plus extra to serve
1 chicken breast (skin on),
  sliced into 3–4 long pieces
80–100g barley couscous
160–200ml hot chicken or
  vegetable stock (optional)
2 preserved lemons
4 dried apricots
small bunch of flat-leaf parsley
small bunch of mint leaves
greens of choice: broad beans,
  peas, broccoli or asparagus all
  work well
small handful of pine nuts,
  toasted
grated zest and juice of
  ½ unwaxed lemon, to serve

Mix the harissa and oil, coat the chicken pieces in the mixture, cover and chill in the fridge for 1 hour (this marinating time isn't essential, but will give the chicken a deeper flavour).

Preheat the grill to medium, or heat a griddle pan over a medium heat. Grill or griddle the marinated chicken pieces for a few minutes on each side until they are cooked through.

Meanwhile, prepare the couscous according to the packet instructions, with hot chicken or vegetable stock, or simply hot water. Cover and set aside while you chop up the preserved lemons and apricots, finely chop the herbs and cook the greens.

Toss the couscous with the preserved lemons, apricots, herbs, pine nuts and greens and place the chicken on top. Drizzle with oil, scatter over the lemon zest and add a spritz of lemon juice.

Serve warm or let it cool and keep it in the fridge for a packed lunch the next day.

Variations:
– Try ras-el-hanout or a mix of the spices from page 48 instead of harissa.
– Make it into more of a salad by adding chopped tomatoes, cucumber and beetroot.
– Try swapping the herbs for dill and basil.
– Vary the nuts by using pistachios, hazelnuts and/or almonds.

Habas y jamon

This Spanish take on 'beans and ham' is quick to prepare and utterly satisfying, with or without a glass of wine on the side. Needless to say, some Pan con Tomate (page 29) is delicious with this dish, or a slice of toasted sourdough to mop up all the juices…

1 tbsp vegetable or light
  olive oil
1 banana shallot or two smaller
  shallots, finely chopped
1 garlic clove, finely chopped
100–120g Spanish ham,
  smoked pancetta or bacon,
  finely chopped
a pinch of pimenton dulce
  (or picante if you like it hot)
250g broad beans, podded
  (when in season use fresh,
  but I use frozen and they're
  fine too)
1–2 tbsp sherry or white
  wine vinegar
sea salt and freshly ground
  black pepper
a generous pinch of chopped
  parsley leaves, to serve
  (optional)

Heat the oil in a skillet or frying pan over a low-medium heat, add the chopped shallot and fry until translucent and soft. Add the chopped garlic and cook for a further minute, then transfer the shallot and garlic to a small bowl. Add the Spanish ham, pancetta or bacon to the pan and fry for a few minutes until it browns nicely. Add the pimenton and turn off the heat.

Meanwhile, bring a pan of water to the boil, add the broad beans and cook for 2–3 minutes until just cooked. Drain in a colander and cool under cold running water to stop them overcooking. Peel the outer skin from the broad beans if you're not a fan, otherwise just add them as they are to the bacon in the skillet or frying pan (back over a low-medium heat) with the shallot and garlic mixture and stir, adding salt and pepper to taste.

Season to taste with the vinegar, to balance out all the flavours, then serve warm, scattered with the parsley (if using), or keep for a room-temperature meal later.

Courgette, lemon and basil pasta

Here's a quick vegetarian pasta dish that can easily be adapted to other greens: try it with asparagus, broccoli or broad beans when you tire of courgette.

100g spaghetti or linguine
  (or pasta of choice)
2 tbsp olive oil
1 banana shallot or 2–3 smaller
  shallots, finely chopped
1 garlic clove, finely chopped
a pinch of chilli flakes
1 courgette, roughly grated
  or chopped
leaves from a few sprigs of basil
grated zest and juice of ½ small
  unwaxed lemon
sea salt and freshly ground
  black pepper
Parmesan cheese, grated,
  to serve
2 tbsp pine nuts, toasted,
  to serve

Bring a medium saucepan of salted water to the boil and cook the pasta according to the packet instructions.

Meanwhile, heat half the olive oil in a separate skillet or frying pan over a low-medium heat, add the shallot and fry for about 5 minutes until soft, then add the garlic and chilli flakes and fry for a further minute. Add the remaining olive oil, tip in the courgette, season with salt and pepper and cook a further 1–2 minutes, just long enough for the courgette to absorb some of the flavour from the garlic, shallot and chilli. Switch off the heat, add the basil leaves and allow the basil to wilt slightly before adding the lemon zest and juice.

Drain the pasta, and if the skillet or frying pan is large enough to hold the spaghetti or linguine, add it while it's draining so you get a little of the pasta water mixing with the courgette. Otherwise, add the courgette mixture to the pasta pan after you've drained the pasta. Stir through and serve hot, with lots of grated Parmesan and the pine nuts scattered on top.

Linguine vongole alle bianco

Of all the seafood pastas I cook, this is the one I love the most – there's something magical about the clatter of clam shells and the simplicity of the cooking process. Quick to make and bursting with flavour, the secret to linguine vongole comes courtesy of chef Francesco Mazzei: don't over-complicate it, and create an emulsion sauce by adding some of the pasta cooking water to the clam sauce for a silky, smooth finish.

175–250g clams, covered in cold
  water with a little salt and
  left for 1 hour
100g linguine or spaghetti
1 tbsp olive oil
1–2 garlic cloves, thinly sliced
1 fresh red chilli, finely chopped
splash of white wine (up to 50ml)
1 small bunch of flat-leaf
  parsley, finely chopped
sea salt and freshly ground
  black pepper (optional)

Drain the clams and rinse them thoroughly with fresh cold water to clean them of sand and grit. Throw away any that remain open if you tap them.

Bring a saucepan full of lightly salted water to the boil and add the pasta.

While the pasta's cooking, heat the olive oil in a separate saucepan over a medium heat. Add the garlic and chilli and fry for a couple of minutes, then add the white wine. Turn up the heat so the alcohol evaporates slightly, then add the clams. Stir and cover the pan with a lid, turn down the heat to medium and cook for a few minutes until all the clams pop open, then add the parsley.

When the pasta is al dente, scoop out an espresso cupful, or a few tablespoons, of the cooking water. Add it to the clams and stir well to create an emulsion with the juices in the pan. Taste and adjust the seasoning (if needed). Add the drained pasta to the pan, mix thoroughly (or do this in the saucepan you cooked the pasta in) and serve hot.

Variations:
– Add a little chopped tomato to the initial stage of cooking. This makes the sauce 'alle rosso' rather than bianco.
– Add lemon zest and a spritz of juice at the end.
– Stirring in a little pat of butter adds richness to the sauce.

Spaghetti carbonara

The dish I always requested for my birthday growing up, spaghetti carbonara still feels like a special treat.

I've pared it back from Mama Johansen's 1980s version, leaving out the cream. Getting a smooth, silky carbonara with no cream follows the same principle as linguine vongole: simply create an emulsion with the fat and some pasta water. It's not 'traditional', but I like Heston Blumenthal's addition of a finely chopped green chilli, but you could leave it out, or use red chilli instead, if you prefer.

Peas are often cited as a good accompaniment but I prefer a side of broccoli, cooked al dente – somehow the dark, cruciferous vegetable pairs better with the deep, savoury flavour of carbonara.

vegetable or light olive oil,
  for frying
50g smoked or unsmoked
  pancetta (or guanciale
  if you can source it), cubed
100–125g spaghetti
1 garlic clove, thinly sliced
1 fresh green chilli, finely
  chopped
1 egg
2–3 tbsp finely grated
  Parmesan cheese, plus extra
  to serve
sea salt and freshly ground
  black pepper

Bring a pan of lightly salted water to the boil.

Heat a little oil in a skillet or frying pan over a medium heat, add the pancetta and fry for a few minutes until golden and crisp around the edges. Add the spaghetti to the boiling water.

Add the garlic and chilli to the frying pan and cook a further minute. Remove from the heat.

In a bowl, combine the egg, grated Parmesan and a good crack of black pepper.

When the spaghetti's al dente, scoop out an espresso cupful, or a few tablespoons,of the pasta cooking water and stir this into the egg and Parmesan mixture to warm it and slightly emulsify the sauce. Drain the spaghetti, return it to the pan, add the egg and Parmesan and toss to coat the spaghetti in the sauce before adding the pancetta, garlic and chilli. Serve with a sprinkle of Parmesan on top.

Variations:
– For a richer sauce, add an extra egg yolk to the egg mixture.
– Substitute the Parmesan for Pecorino Romano.

Crispy halloumi with watermelon, mint and cucumber

Inspired by the eastern Mediterranean, this simple dish hits the spot when watermelon comes into season. I love it on a blisteringly hot day, as the melon and cucumber are ideal for rehydration, and the salty punch of grilled halloumi is so satisfying.

100g halloumi cheese, cut
  into bite-sized cubes
olive oil, plus extra to serve
  (optional)
1–2 watermelon wedges,
  cut into similar-sized cubes
⅓ cucumber, cut into ribbons
  with a vegetable peeler
1 shallot or 1 small red onion,
  thinly sliced and placed in a
  bowl of iced water for a few
  minutes
handful of mint leaves
freshly ground black pepper
drizzle of balsamic vinegar or
  pomegranate molasses

Coat the halloumi cubes in a little olive oil. Heat a skillet or frying pan over a medium heat, add the halloumi and fry for a few minutes until the cubes are golden brown and crispy on each side.

Scatter the watermelon cubes, cucumber ribbons and shallot or onion slices (drained of the iced water) in a shallow bowl or on a dinner plate and place the grilled halloumi cubes around the salad. Garnish with lots of mint leaves and season with pepper. A drizzle of balsamic vinegar or pomegranate molasses adds a nice hit of acidity, and a little extra-virgin olive oil adds gloss.

Eat.

Variation: Instead of halloumi, try feta, queso fresco (Spanish fresh cheese) or plain cottage cheese for a milder flavour (they wouldn't need to be fried).

Leftovers: If you have a lot of leftover watermelon, try making a refreshing watermelon, mint and lime ice crush in the blender, or a watermelon, tomato and olive salad.

Late-night miso ramen

Rather than diving into a packet of crisps, instant or quick-cook ramen is ideal when you've been out late and fancy a bite to eat before bedtime.

150g packet miso ramen
  noodles (or plain noodles)
handful of frozen peas, or any
  vegetables you have lurking
  in the fridge (carrots, sugarsnap
  peas, corn, bean sprouts, finely
  shredded cabbage, courgette,
  etc.)
1 egg
1 tbsp red or brown miso paste
  (if using plain noodles)
1 fresh green chilli, sliced
1 spring onion, sliced and
  placed in a bowl of iced water
  for a few minutes
a generous pinch of black or
  white sesame seeds
toasted sesame oil, to taste
Japanese dried nori seaweed,
  to serve (optional)

Cook the ramen noodles according to the packet instructions, adding the frozen peas (or whichever veg you opt for) to the pan so they cook at the same time. Cook the egg by poaching it in the broth (whisk it in a bowl first then pour it into the broth or crack it in), boiling it whole in a separate pan, or giving it a quick fry.

Add the miso paste to the noodle cooking liquid (if cooking plain noodles) and stir through. Remove from the heat and garnish with the chilli, drained spring onion, sesame seeds, sesame oil and any other toppings you like. The egg goes on last if you cooked it separately, along with the seaweed (if using).

Variations: You can really play around with this recipe, adding all manner of ingredients. These work particularly well – assorted pickles, citrus, herbs, mushrooms, kimchi, sriracha sauce, coconut milk or cream, peanut butter and Korean gochujang paste.

Leftovers: Add leftover roast meat such as chicken, shellfish such as prawns, or tofu (adding the crispy tofu from page 65 really ramps up this dish).

Crispy tofu with kimchi, cucumber and spring onion

Though bland, tofu is easy to fry and crisps up beautifully. I love the contrast of textures and flavours here – you can play around with the dressing to your own taste; the key is to pair the fried tofu with something quite savoury.

150g firm tofu, cut into
 roughly 2.5cm cubes
2 tbsp cornflour
1 egg
1 tbsp mix of black and white
 sesame seeds, plus extra
 sesame seeds (white, black,
 or a mix of both) to garnish
vegetable oil, for frying
½ cucumber, peeled lengthways
 into ribbons
2 tbsp kimchi, chopped
1 spring onion, thinly sliced
a pinch of chilli powder or
 cayenne (optional)

For the miso dressing
1 tsp brown or red miso paste
1 tbsp mirin
1 tbsp toasted sesame oil
1 tsp delicate honey (such as acacia)
sea salt and freshly ground
 black pepper

Carefully place the tofu cubes on a few sheets of kitchen paper and cover them with more paper, to remove any excess moisture. Put the cornflour in a bowl, lightly beat the egg in another bowl, and put the mixed sesame seeds in a third bowl.

Combine the dressing ingredients in a bowl and season to taste with salt and pepper.

Pour vegetable oil into a medium saucepan to a depth of 2.5cm and place over a medium heat. Heat the oil to 160°C. If you don't have a thermometer, test the oil by dropping in a cube of stale bread – if it sizzles, the oil is hot enough.

Dip the tofu pieces into the cornflour, then dip them in the egg, then gently roll them in the seeds (they don't have to be completely covered).

Fry the tofu for 4–6 minutes (in batches if necessary, to avoid overcrowding the pan), turning them frequently, until golden and crispy all over. Using a slotted spoon, remove the tofu and place on clean kitchen paper to absorb any excess oil.

Arrange the cucumber ribbons on a plate or in a shallow bowl and drizzle over most of the dressing. Add the kimchi and spring onion and scatter over some sesame seeds. Finally, add the crispy tofu and lightly dust with chilli or cayenne if you wish. Drizzle over the remaining dressing.

Variation: Try other greens instead of cucumber, such as par-boiled sugarsnap peas, broad beans, asparagus, broccoli, spinach or courgette.

One-pan Wonders

—

Simple roasted salmon

As I've mentioned elsewhere, we Scandis like to treat our seafood with as little fuss and embellishment as possible – this is one such example. A good piece of roasted salmon can then be spun into any number of dishes.

500g fillet of salmon, skin on
butter
1 lemon, halved
sea salt and freshly ground
　black pepper

Preheat the oven to 180°C/gas mark 4 and line a roasting dish with baking parchment.

Place the salmon in the roasting dish skin-side down and season it generously with salt and pepper, then dot about 6 pats of butter over the top (or melt the butter and brush it over the fish if you prefer. As an impatient cook I just dot it over the salmon).

Roast the fish in the oven for about 20 minutes, or until the flesh is pretty much opaque and cooked all the way through.

Remove the fish from the oven and squeeze lemon juice all over the top, leaving it to soak into the fish for a few minutes before eating.

Keep the remaining fish for a salad the next day, a delicious salmon sandwich or to enjoy at room temperature with some freshly cooked broccoli, assorted greens and rice, noodles or potatoes.

Variation: Make a zingy spread for the top of the salmon by combining 2 tablespoons wholegrain mustard, 1 tablespoon horseradish sauce, 1 teaspoon demerara sugar, 1 tinned anchovy fillet, 1 teaspoon fennel seeds/coriander (seeds or ground)/ pimenton and slather this mixture all over the fish before cooking. Squeeze lots of lemon over the fish before serving, as above.

Mussels, fennel and wine

One of the most economical types of seafood you can eat, mussels are sometimes a forgotten source of joy for solo cooks. More's the pity as they're plentiful and nutritious. Although this is a fast dish to cook, be aware that mussels require a little attention beforehand.

500g mussels, rinsed under
  cold running water and scrubbed
1 tbsp vegetable oil
1 fennel bulb, finely chopped
  (reserve the fennel fronds
  to garnish at the end)
1 shallot, finely chopped
1 garlic clove, thinly sliced
1 small bay leaf
50–75ml dry white wine
25g butter
grated zest of ½ unwaxed lemon
  and a spritz of the juice
sea salt (optional) and freshly
  ground black pepper
bread, to serve (I like a big,
  crunchy baguette)

Tap any mussels with open shells. If they remain open after a few minutes, discard them. To remove the 'beard' that pokes out of the shell, hold the mussel and yank the beard out in the direction of the mussel's hinge. Place the mussels in a bowl of cold water for an hour or so.

Heat the oil in a medium saucepan over a low-medium heat, add the fennel and fry for 5 minutes, then add the shallot. Fry for 1 minute, then add the garlic and fry for a further minute. Add the bay leaf and wine. Crank up the heat, bring the wine to a simmer and add a crack of pepper. Finally, add the mussels and cover. Cook over a medium-high heat until the mussels steam open: small ones will only need a couple of minutes, larger ones 3–4 minutes. Transfer the mussels to a bowl and whisk the butter into the pan to emulsify the sauce. Add the lemon zest and juice, taste the sauce and season it accordingly – the mussels will release quite a lot of salinity, so you may not need to add salt.

Discard any closed mussels and serve in a shallow bowl with the sauce, scattered with the fennel fronds, along with whatever bread you fancy.

Variations:
– Substitute the wine for dry sherry.
– Add a heaped dessertspoonful of crème fraîche or double cream to the sauce once you've removed the mussels from the pan.
– Add saffron, chilli or harissa for an extra kick.
– Add chopped parsley, thyme or basil, just before serving.

Grilled citrus, chilli and vegetable medley

Whenever you crave a plate of vegetables this is the recipe to turn to. I love how you can spin the leftovers into a variety of dishes: soup, a couscous salad, wraps for lunch and a simple antipasti platter when you don't feel like eating a hot meal.

2 red onions or shallots, cut into bite-sized chunks
1 courgette, cut into bite-sized chunks
1 aubergine, cut into bite-sized chunks
1 red pepper, halved, deseeded and cut into bite-sized chunks
1 unwaxed lemon, quartered if small or cut into eight pieces if large
2 garlic cloves (or more if you're a garlic fiend), finely chopped or thinly sliced
2 sprigs of thyme or rosemary
olive oil, for drizzling
balsamic vinegar, for drizzling
chilli flakes, to taste
sea salt and freshly ground black pepper
crusty bread, to serve

Preheat the grill to medium and line a large roasting tray with a sheet of baking parchment (this isn't essential but it helps keep the tray clean).

Scatter the vegetable chunks and lemon pieces in the tray and add the garlic. Tuck the thyme or rosemary sprigs slightly under the vegetables so the herbs don't burn under the grill. Drizzle generously with a few tablespoons of olive oil and a few splashes of balsamic vinegar then season with salt, pepper and chilli flakes.

Grill for 10 minutes, remove the tray and gently toss the vegetables before returning the tray to the grill. Keep grilling for a further 10 minutes, or until most of the vegetables have taken on a decent amount of colour and are cooked through.

Remove from the grill and pick out the grilled lemon. Smoosh them into crusty bread and eat alongside the vegetable medley.

Serve immediately or leave to cool and serve as a side to any dish you like, such as the roasted sea bass on page 38.

Leftovers: Toss leftover veg into the Grilled Harissa Chicken salad (page 51), serve with Courgette, Lemon and Basil Pasta (page 54), in the frittata (page 74) or as a filling in the quesadilla (page 162).

Galentine's Day frittata

Fans of US sitcom *Parks and Recreation* will be familiar with 'Galentine's Day' – a day when ladies celebrate ladies. For those unfamiliar with 'the best day of the year': it takes place annually on 13th February, there is a cornucopia of breakfast foods to feast on and really it's an excuse to get your favourite women together over frittatas and waffles.

Cook this frittata on any day of the year, and when you do, remember to salute the gals in your life!

butter, for frying
1 tsp olive oil
handful of small button or
  chestnut mushrooms, cleaned
  and quartered or thickly sliced
2 spring onions, thinly sliced
3 medium eggs or 2 very
  large eggs, lightly beaten
handful or small bowl of
  Grilled Citrus, Chilli and
  Vegetable Medley (page 72)
chopped herbs of choice
  (parsley and chives are great
  in this)
1–2 tbsp grated cheese of
  choice (Parmesan, Gruyere,
  Comte, aged Jarlsberg,
  Cheddar... whatever you
  fancy)
sea salt and freshly ground
  black pepper

Preheat the oven to 220°C/gas mark 7 or preheat the grill to medium.

Heat 1 tablespoon of butter with the oil in an ovenproof skillet or frying pan over a medium heat and once the butter is foaming, add the mushrooms with a little salt and pepper and fry for about 5 minutes, or until they're golden brown and have lost their sponginess. Add the spring onion and cook for a further 1–2 minutes, then add a knob more butter to the pan, pour in the eggs, scatter in the roasted vegetables, herbs and lightly season again with salt and pepper. Stir.

Sprinkle the cheese evenly on top and bake in the oven for 5–8 minutes, or place under the grill for 3–5 minutes until the middle of the frittata is puffed up and golden brown.

Serve warm, preferably straight from the pan.

Baked sweet potato with feta, herbs and tomatoes

A baked potato offers real comfort, and I find the cheering sight of a bright, orange sweet potato to be particularly pleasing. Sweet potatoes take their time to fully bake through, especially the large ones, but they are definitely worth the wait. Pairing them with savoury ingredients tempers their natural sweetness, making this into a complete meal.

1 medium sweet potato, skin on but thoroughly scrubbed
handful of cherry or baby plum tomatoes, halved
olive oil, for drizzling
leaves from a few sprigs of thyme or oregano
100g feta cheese, cubed
a few pitted green and black olives (optional)
sea salt and freshly ground black pepper

Preheat the oven to 200°C/gas mark 6.

Pierce the sweet potato skin a few times all over and place it in a medium roasting dish in the oven for 30 minutes (if you prefer less washing up, line the roasting dish with a sheet of baking parchment).

Remove the dish from the oven, add the tomatoes, drizzle them with a little olive oil and season with salt and pepper. Put the tray back in the oven and continue to roast for a further 30 minutes, or until the sweet potato is fully baked through.

Remove the dish from the oven and slice the sweet potato in half lengthways (still in the dish). Open it like a book and use a fork to slightly smash the flesh so it fluffs up a little. Place the herbs and feta cubes over the top, along with the olives (if using) and roast for a further 10 minutes (take the tomatoes out of the dish if they're ready, or leave them in if they're still a little raw), or until the feta turns a shade of golden brown and softens.

Eat while warm, along with a simple green salad if you wish.

Variation: Use Parmesan or any other favourite cheese instead of feta.

Polish dill pickle soup

There's a time and a place for store-bought soup when you're short on time. I find cooking soup, however, to be therapeutic: rummaging through the kitchen, chucking whatever is lurking in the fridge and cupboard into a pan with stock and bringing to a gentle simmer. Often the best soups are the ones that have no recipe and are just an assembly of good ingredients, made while tuning in to a podcast.

This dish, however, *is* an actual recipe, and comes courtesy of food writer Marlena Spieler who shares my love of dill pickles. It's a wholesome mix of vegetables, potatoes and cream but what really adds punch is the dill pickle juice. It's an unusual combination of otherwise modest ingredients, and makes a change from good old cream of tomato…

Makes 3–4 portions

1 litre vegetable or chicken stock
8 waxy potatoes, halved
2 carrots, thickly sliced
2 celery sticks, thickly sliced
1 leek, thickly sliced
3 garlic cloves, roughly chopped
2 dill pickles, roughly chopped
  (ogorky kishonie, from Polish
  delis, are the best and akin to
  American, Russian or kosher
  dill pickles – you can also use
  vinegar-brined pickles)
125ml pickle brine, or to taste
75–100ml double cream
sea salt and freshly ground
  black pepper
1 small bunch of dill, finely
  chopped, to serve
good dark rye bread slices,
  to serve

Put the stock, potatoes, carrots, celery, leek, garlic and half the chopped dill pickles in a medium saucepan. Bring to the boil, then turn down the heat to low and simmer for 15 minutes until the vegetables are tender.

Add the remaining pickles and pickle brine, taste and season if you think it needs it. Set aside a few portions to chill for the next couple of days or freeze, then add the double cream to the soup you're planning to eat straight away, stirring it first in a separate bowl with a little of the soup liquid, then returning it to the pan (if you add the cream directly to the hot soup it may curdle).

Garnish with the fresh dill and season to taste. Serve hot with rye bread on the side.

Variations:
– Use sour cream or crème fraîche instead of double cream.
– Chuck in any root vegetables you might have: swede, turnip, celeriac and parsley root are all great in this soup.

Bolognese ragù sauce

Opinion is quite sharply divided about what constitutes a real bolognese ragù. Plenty of purists will claim that it has to be cooked a certain way, or contain certain ingredients. Truth be told, who really cares? No two bolognese ragù sauces are ever the same, and the best ones I've made have often been conjured up simply by using whatever's in the fridge, freezer and store-cupboard.

This recipe is a basic formula which you can tweak to your own taste. It should be beefy, intensely savoury and provide instant comfort in times of need, exhaustion or when you have an overwhelming desire for something ferrous. Scale the recipe down by half, or double it for large-scale batch cooking, but beware that the cooking times may alter.

Save yourself some chopping time by using a 500g bag of frozen soffritto mix, defrosted, if you like.

Makes about 6 portions

25g lightly salted butter
75g smoked pancetta or
  bacon, cubed
1 white or red onion, finely
  chopped
2 carrots, finely chopped
2 celery sticks, finely chopped
500g beef mince
nutmeg, for grating
150ml red or white wine (plus
  another glass for the cook!)
500ml beef or chicken stock
1 x 400g tin of plum tomatoes
  (or the same weight of
  fresh tomatoes, chopped)
½ tsp dried oregano
1 bay leaf
sea salt and freshly ground
  black pepper

Melt the butter in a medium-large ovenproof casserole over a medium heat, add the pancetta or bacon and cook for a few minutes until starting to crisp up and the fat is rendered. Add the vegetables and cook for a further 5–10 minutes until they soften (the cooking time will depend on the size of your pan).

Preheat the oven to 150°C/gas mark 1.

Form the beef mince into 4 balls and season them generously with salt and pepper. Push the vegetables and pancetta to one side of the pan (or transfer them to a bowl), add the balls of mince and fry them for about 10 minutes, turning them so they caramelise all over and take on a good amount of colour, then roughly break up the balls and stir them together with the vegetables and pancetta (add them back to the casserole if you transferred them to a bowl while frying the beef). Season with a little freshly grated nutmeg.

Pour in the wine and cook for a few minutes to allow the alcohol to evaporate, then add the stock, tomatoes, oregano and bay leaf.

Season with a little salt and pepper (if the stock is already seasoned, hold back on the salt) and heat through – if necessary, add a little more stock to cover the meat. Scrunch up a piece of baking parchment then un-scrunch it and place it on top of the sauce. Cover the pan with a lid and place it in the oven. Bake the bolognese for 45 minutes, then remove the pan from the oven, lift the lid and check if the sauce is thickening – it should simmer gently, not boil like mad. Return it to the oven and bake for a further 45 minutes. I find its texture is ideal at this stage but if you like a really thick sauce, pass the bolognese through a sieve into a clean pan, reserving the solid ingredients in a bowl, and reduce the liquid by half.

Taste and adjust the seasoning if necessary. Eat with pasta of choice, and freeze whatever you don't use in solo batches.

Variations: Crikey, they're endless…
– Milk is often added along with the stock and/or wine but I find the butter adds real depth of flavour and some delicious dairy fat to the sauce.
– Many like to add 50–100g chopped chicken livers to their bolognese, after frying off the mince.
– My mother adds chopped green pepper to the soffritto mix (a trick she picked up from my grandmother, who randomly picked it up from someone in Hong Kong. I know, me neither. But it works!) and much more wine.
– If I don't have wine in the house I'll add a splash of brandy to deglaze and then a little wine vinegar or balsamic vinegar for extra acidity.
– Heston Blumenthal adds a star anise to his bolognese, which really brings out the flavour of the beef. You can chuck in Worcestershire sauce, ketchup, anchovy sauce and all manner of umami-rich ingredients if you have them in your cupboard, just do so sparingly as they're all highly concentrated in flavour. You still want to taste the beef and vegetables at the end of the cooking process.

Beef, shiitake mushroom and broccoli stir-fry

A nourishing meal both rich in flavour and easy to prepare, I find stir-fries are often the best standby for those moments when you're lacking inspiration as you return home from school or work.

1 tbsp vegetable or
  sunflower oil
1 tsp soy sauce, plus extra
  to taste
1 tsp rice vinegar (or white
  wine/cider vinegar), plus
  extra to taste
1 tsp grated fresh root ginger
2 garlic cloves, finely grated
1 tsp honey or brown sugar
120g beef (sirloin, flank and
  skirt all work well), cut across
  the grain into strips
handful of shiitake
  mushrooms, sliced
4 tenderstem broccoli stalks,
  chopped into 2.5cm pieces
1 fresh red chilli, sliced
1 spring onion, sliced
toasted sesame oil, to taste
sesame seeds, to garnish
egg or rice noodles, cooked
  according to the packet
  instructions (optional),
  to serve

Mix the oil, teaspoon of soy sauce, teaspoon of vinegar, ginger, garlic and honey or brown sugar in a bowl, then add the beef strips to a bowl. Leave it to marinate for a few minutes so the beef doesn't dry out when you cook it. If the beef is quite a tough cut, leave it to marinate for longer in the fridge (you can do this the night before or morning of the day you plan to cook it).

Place a wok over a high heat. You'll know it's hot enough and ready for stir-frying when you flick a little water into the pan and it immediately evaporates. Add the marinated beef and cook it for a few minutes, tossing and stirring it constantly so none of it burns. Remove the beef from the pan. Add a little more oil if the wok is dry, add the mushrooms and broccoli and fry for a minute or two, tossing frequently, then add the chilli and spring onion. Stir a couple more times, then taste. Season the stir-fry with sesame oil, soy sauce and vinegar to bring out all the flavours of the dish and serve hot, garnished with lots of sesame seeds on egg or rice noodles (if you wish).

Roast cauliflower with chilli, garlic and thyme

As any good cook will tell you, this is a ridiculously easy way to transform what is otherwise quite a bland vegetable: roasting cauliflower brings out its sweet nuttiness, and I love this dish on nights when I just want to veg out (sorry, couldn't resist) in front of the TV.

1 large head of cauliflower,
  broken into roughly
  equal-sized florets, stalk
  trimmed and chopped
1 fresh red chilli, thickly sliced
2 garlic cloves, sliced
3 sprigs of thyme, plus extra
  leaves to serve (optional)
olive oil
balsamic or sherry vinegar
sea salt and freshly ground
  black pepper

Preheat the oven to 200°C/gas mark 6.

Put the florets of cauliflower and chopped stalk in a bowl with the chilli, garlic and thyme sprigs, and stir. Drizzle over a glug of oil and season with salt and pepper. Tip it all into a roasting dish or tray and drizzle a little vinegar over the top. Roast in the oven for 25 minutes until caramelised, turning the florets halfway through cooking so they cook evenly. If the florets are large, you may need to cook them for longer.

Remove the cauliflower from the oven and eat it as it is, scattered with fresh thyme leaves (if you wish), or alongside cooked rice, lentils, beans or with grilled meat.

Variations:
– Chop up an unwaxed lemon, rind and all, and add it to the mixture instead of the vinegar.
– Toss the florets in ½ teaspoon each of curry powder, garam masala and cumin seeds before roasting.
– Mix some harissa, ras-el-hanout or white or red miso paste with the oil.
– Swap the cauliflower for chopped sweet potato, parsnip, celeriac or swede (cooking time may vary).
– While I'm not so keen on bland cauliflower cheese sauces, I do like adding some grated Gruyere, Cheddar, Parmesan or crumbled blue cheese over the roasted cauliflower about 5 minutes before removing it from the oven.
– Add radicchio, chicory and toasted nuts to turn it into a simple hot or cold salad.

Cuban-inspired rice and beans

Here's a dish, variously known as *arroz congri* or *moros y cristianos*, that really is more than the sum of its parts: smoky bacon and wholesome black beans are married with warming spices and given a lift from sprightly green pepper. Nourishing and delicious comfort food at its finest.

vegetable oil, for frying
75g smoked bacon, pancetta,
   or chorizo cubes
1 red onion, finely chopped
1 green pepper, finely chopped
   (the same size as the onion)
1 garlic clove, finely chopped
½ tsp ground cumin
1 x 400g tin of black beans,
   drained and rinsed
400ml beef, chicken or
   vegetable stock
½ tsp tomato purée
1 tbsp vinegar
1 bay leaf
a pinch of dried oregano and/
   or pimenton dulce/picante
60–90g brown or white rice
chopped fresh flat-leaf parsley,
   oregano or coriander, to garnish
sea salt and freshly ground
   black pepper

Heat a little oil in a medium saucepan over a medium heat, add the bacon, pancetta or chorizo and fry until it starts to crisp up. Scoop out with a slotted spoon and set it aside.

Add the onion and green pepper to the same pan and fry for 5 minutes, or until soft, then turn down the heat to low-medium, add the garlic and cook for a further minute. Add the cumin and fry for a few seconds, then add the black beans, stock, tomato purée, vinegar, bay leaf, oregano, pimenton (if using) and the bacon, pancetta or chorizo. Turn up the heat and cook for about 20 minutes, or until the mixture have thickened and half of the liquid has evaporated. Season to taste.

Meanwhile, cook the rice according to the packet instructions, fluffing up the grains with a fork when cooked.

Serve the rice with the beans, garnished with fresh herbs (saving half for lunch tomorrow – it's delicious eaten cold in a wrap with avocado, lime and some coriander). Typically, the beans are folded into the rice but I prefer to serve the beans on top. It's up to you…

Variations:
– Swap the green pepper for red pepper, fennel or a classic soffritto mix of onions, carrots and celery.
– Add more spices and herbs if you wish.
– Add a spoonful of crème fraîche or Greek yoghurt just before serving, and plate up with a wedge of lemon or lime.

Make
Ahead

—

Vanilla overnight oats

Otherwise known by *mitteleuropeans* as Bircher Müsli, the method of soaking oats overnight was invented by Swiss physician Dr. Maximilian Bircher-Benner at the turn of the last century. I've tried making it so many ways over the years, even with the delicious addition of cream, but frankly that just transforms your breakfast into dessert, so I've streamlined it to this simple method. It's a fresh yet delicately sweet version of Bircher that I tend to favour during summertime, but it can be prepared any time of the year for quick and easy breakfasts.

Makes enough for 5 weekday breakfasts

250g jumbo oats (toasted or straight out of the packet – it's up to you)
250ml almond milk (the Rude Health brand is best)
200ml whole milk
2 green apples, roughly grated or finely chopped
2 tbsp Greek yoghurt
1 tsp vanilla extract or the nib of a vanilla pod, split to help it release its flavour

To serve (one – or a mixture of – the following)
fresh berries
chopped banana
sliced peach
flaxseeds
dried fruit
toasted nuts

Combine all the ingredients in a 1-litre glass preserving jar or medium bowl and scrunch them together using a fork or spoon so everything is thoroughly mixed.

Cover, place in the fridge and leave overnight. I find this keeps from Monday to Friday just fine.

When you're ready to serve the oats, dollop a helping into a bowl and scatter with fruit, nuts, seeds or anything else you fancy.

Pumpkin, Cheddar and fennel seed quick-bread

Savoury quick-breads are more common across the Atlantic and I have fond memories of eating cornbreads and nut breads when I spent summers in New England. Mixed together within minutes, this loaf makes the most of pumpkin which is readily available in the autumn. It's delicious on its own for a savoury brunch, or alongside a soup, stew or a salad.

175g sprouted (or regular) wholemeal flour

150g sprouted (or regular) spelt flour

50g jumbo oats

50g flaxseeds

2 tbsp fennel seeds

1½ tsp baking powder

½ tsp bicarbonate of soda

½ tsp sea salt

¼ tsp cayenne (optional, if you want it to be spicy)

275g pumpkin purée (tinned is great, or use some leftover roast pumpkin if you have it)

100g Greek yoghurt

25g butter, melted, plus extra for greasing (if needed)

2 eggs, beaten

1 tbsp wholegrain mustard (or mustard of choice)

100g mature Cheddar cheese, roughly grated, plus about 30g extra for the top of the bread

Preheat the oven to 190°C/gas mark 5 and lightly grease or line a 900g loaf tin.

Sift the flours into a large bowl, add the rest of the dry ingredients and stir to evenly distribute the raising agents. Mix all the liquid ingredients together (including the mustard) in a separate bowl or in the pan you melted the butter in.

Make a well in the dry ingredients and add the wet ingredients and grated cheese. Working quickly, fold everything together about 12 times in a figure-of-eight motion (don't overwork the mixture). Pour the mixture into the loaf tin, scatter the extra cheese evenly on top and bake for about 45 minutes, or until the bread feels firm to the touch, is well risen and sounds hollow when you remove it from the tin and tap the bottom.

Remove the bread from the tin and allow it to cool on a wire rack, but try to resist cutting a slice while it's still warm – I'd wager it's almost impossible! What you don't use, simply slice and freeze for another day.

Variations:
– Swap fennel seeds for sage, rosemary or thyme.
– A teaspoon of Marmite (leave out the sea salt) gives the bread an extra layer of flavour.
– Try blue cheese, Parmesan or a nutty cheese such as Comte, Jarlsberg or Appenzeller in place of the Cheddar.

Sprouted multigrain soda bread

Few things say it's the weekend like baking a loaf of bread. This sprouted version, replete with nutty, wholesome flavours, is like child's play for bread bakers. No kneading, no proving, no fuss at all. I've adapted a dark chocolate version from my *Scandilicious Baking* book, with a few added ingredients inspired by a superb bread recipe my friends Camilla and Nick Barnard developed for their range of Rude Health sprouted flours. I find this bread more digestible than soda bread made with conventional flours, but if you don't have any trouble digesting regular flour, just use that instead of the sprouted kind.

250g sprouted spelt flour
250g sprouted wholemeal flour
100g jumbo oats or sprouted oats
50g flaxseed or mixed seeds
  of choice
1 tbsp cocoa powder
1½ tsp bicarbonate of soda
1 tsp sea salt
500ml buttermilk
2 tbsp treacle (or 1 tbsp
  treacle and 1 tbsp plain
  honey)
a little oil, for greasing

Preheat the oven to 200°C/gas mark 6 and lightly oil or line a baking tray.

Combine the flours, oats, seeds, cocoa powder, bicarbonate of soda and salt in a large bowl. Make a well in the middle and add the buttermilk and treacle (or treacle and honey). Stir with a large spoon for a minute or so until you have quite a sticky dough. Turn the dough out on to a lightly oiled work surface and lightly oil your hands. Work quickly to form the dough into a round shape. Place the dough on the baking tray, oil the large spoon and press a cross into the dough (this is traditional, and helps the bread cook through). Bake for 45 minutes, or until the bread sounds hollow when tapped on the top and bottom. It should be caramel-brown and smell nutty and delicious.

Remove from the oven and leave to cool on a wire rack. The bread will keep in an airtight container or paper bag for a few days. You can freeze slices for toasting at a later date.

Variations:
– Add nuts and a handful of chopped dried fruit such as figs, cranberries, sour cherries and apricots to the bread mixture.
– If you prefer a slightly lighter texture, substitute one of the wholemeal flours for the same quantity of plain flour.

Peach freezer jam

Give this recipe a try when you have a glut of peaches during summertime. Although we didn't have an abundance of peaches growing in Norway, my grandparents always had fields of strawberries so we made a freezer jam with them; this recipe is merely an adaptation of that method.

I find that by not cooking the peaches you retain their flavour far better, and there's less hassle in having to cook the mixture until it sets. Think of this more as a peach compote, a cheering reminder of golden sunshine and carefree summer days when you take out a batch in deepest, darkest midwinter.

2kg ripe peaches
300g fructose (fruit sugar)
  or 450g caster or jam sugar
juice of 1 lemon
1–2 sachets of pectin (13–26g)
  (optional but it does help
  thicken the freezer jam)

Plunge the peaches into a heatproof bowl of just-boiled water for 1 minute, then drain and peel away the skins. Quarter the peaches, remove the stones, and slice the quarters in half so each peach is cut into eight wedges. Place in a large bowl and sprinkle in the remaining ingredients. Stir with a large metal spoon until the peaches start to macerate and some of their juice oozes out (this can take anything from a couple of minutes to 10–15 minutes). Keep going until the mixture is glossy and juicy but stop before the fruit starts to break down. Transfer the mixture into freezable tubs or boxes, cover, label and freeze for up to a year.

Take a tub or box out of the freezer the night before you want to use it and defrost it in the fridge or on the kitchen surface for a faster defrost. It keeps for about 5 days in the fridge once thawed. Peach jam is excellent on toast, but also makes a fab topping for porridge, Greek yoghurt or the base for a cheat's dessert, such as the Knickerbocker Glory on page 178.

Variations:
– Add a few teaspoons of vanilla extract or the seeds of a vanilla pod to the peach mixture while it's macerating.
– Add herbs such as finely chopped rosemary, mint, thyme or basil to the peach mixture while it's macerating.

Beef, porter and barley stew

Affectionately known as The Great British Stew in our family, this winter warmer requires only a little preparation and a few hours in the oven. Barley thickens the broth and adds a wonderful chewiness to the dish, but you can leave it out if you prefer. As is always the case with a stew, this tastes even better the next day.

Makes about hearty 6 portions

1kg stewing cut of beef (shin, skirt or chuck), cut into 2.5cm cubes and patted dry

3–4 tbsp light olive oil or vegetable oil

5 banana shallots or 3 medium red onions, peeled and roughly chopped

500ml beef stock

500ml porter or stout (taste it – it shouldn't be too bitter)

200g pearl barley

1 tbsp Worcestershire sauce

1 tbsp tomato puree

1 bay leaf

1 small bunch of flat-leaf parsley, stalks and leaves

2 medium carrots, cut into chunks

sea salt and freshly ground black pepper

Preheat the oven to 150°C/gas mark 1.

Season the beef. Heat 1 tablespoon of the oil in a cast-iron casserole over a medium heat and fry the beef in batches (2–3 batches, depending on the size of your pan) for a few minutes until brown all over, being careful not to let it burn.

Transfer each batch to a bowl and add water to the pan to deglaze it (to a depth of about 1cm). Pass the deglazing liquid through a sieve into the bowl with the cooked beef – it adds flavour to the stew – and repeat the browning and deglazing process then add a final tablespoon of oil to the pan, add the shallots or onions and sweat for 8–10 minutes until translucent. Add the remaining ingredients (including parsley stalks), except the browned beef, carrots and parsley leaves. Bring to the boil, add the beef and check that everything is covered by liquid. If necessary, top up with a little more stock or water. Cover the liquid with a scrunched up and unfolded piece of baking parchment, then top with a lid. Transfer to the oven for 2 hours, checking on the beef after 1 hour – the liquid should be simmering, not boiling vigorously. If it's boiling, turn the oven down by 20–30°C. After 2 hours, add the carrots and return to the oven for a final hour.

Serve the stew warm, sprinkled with chopped parsley leaves, or chill overnight and enjoy it the next day. Freeze the rest in individual portions.

A simple roast chicken

One of the most evocative dishes for cooks and eaters alike is a classic roast chicken. Few things are as sublime as the scent of a chook browning and crisping in a hot oven, and naturally everyone has an opinion on what makes the perfect roast bird.

Consider this simple method a primer, rather than the ultimate roast chicken recipe. You can find further inspiration from brilliant cooks and writers such as Diana Henry, Simon Hopkinson, Catherine Phipps, Felicity Cloake, Nigel Slater, Ina Garten (aka The Barefoot Contessa) and Fiona Beckett – they all give great advice on roasting a chicken. (Pictured overleaf.)

1 good-quality, free-range chicken (1.4–1.8kg)
1 small onion (red or yellow) or a banana shallot, peeled and halved
2 garlic cloves, peeled and halved
1 small, unwaxed lemon, halved
herbs of choice (e.g. thyme, rosemary, bay, sage, parsley stalks)
a little soft butter or olive oil (optional)
sea salt and freshly ground black pepper

Remove the chicken from its packaging a few hours before cooking so it can dry out a little. Keep it in the fridge like this overnight if you like, but take it out 45 minutes before roasting.

Preheat the oven to 220°C/gas mark 7.

Season the cavity of the chicken, then stuff it with the onion, garlic, lemon and herbs. Season the skin all over and place the bird in a roasting dish or oven tray that keeps it snug. Smear butter or oil over the chicken if you like, but I find it's just as delicious without.

Roast for 20 minutes, then turn the heat down to 180°C/gas mark 4 and roast for a further 30–45 minutes, or until the juices run clear. Remove and let it rest for at least 15 minutes, in the roasting dish or on a board that can catch the delicious juices.

I like to savour the brown meat and crispy wings straight away, and keep the white meat for sandwiches or salads the next day. Don't forget that the carcass makes a tasty stock (page 197).

Leftovers: Use leftover meat in a quesadilla (page 162), in a salad such as Succotash Salad (page 49), in my Polish Dill Pickle Soup (page 77), or fold into the Spiced Dhal (page 100).

Spiced dhal

The first time I had a really transformative bowl of dhal was courtesy of author and television judge/critic Simon Majumdar. While he calls his recipe 'life-saving dahl' (LSD) I can't claim mine has any hallucinogenic properties, but it does work wonders when you're feeling a little low, beset by the sniffles or just exhausted by the pace of modern life.

Makes 6–8 portions

3 tbsp ghee or vegetable oil
3 garlic cloves, finely chopped
1 fresh green chilli, finely chopped
1 tsp grated fresh root ginger
1 small cinnamon stick
4 green cardamom pods, bruised
500g red lentils, rinsed
1.2 litres water or vegetable/
  chicken stock
1 x 400g tin of plum tomatoes
  (or 400g fresh tomatoes,
  roughly chopped)
2 tbsp ghee or vegetable oil
1 tsp curry powder or garam masala
1 tsp black mustard or nigella seeds
1 tsp ground turmeric
1 tsp cumin seeds
1 tsp coriander seeds
sea salt and freshly ground
  black pepper

To serve
handful of baby spinach,
1–2 eggs
½ small unwaxed lemon
naan bread

Warm 1 tablespoon of the ghee or oil in a large saucepan over a medium heat, add the garlic, chilli and ginger and fry for 30 seconds, then add the cinnamon and cardamom and fry for a further 30 seconds until aromatic. Add the lentils and pour over the water or stock. Bring to the boil, turn down the heat and simmer for 20 minutes, skimming off any scum if necessary. Add the tomatoes, breaking them up with a wooden spoon if using tinned. Cook for 25–30 minutes, or until the lentils are really soft and the mixture has thickened. Add more liquid if it needs it and season to taste. Remove from the heat and discard the cinnamon and cardamom pods.

Heat the remaining ghee or oil in a frying pan over a low-medium heat. Add the remaining spices and fry for a minute or so until they smell fragrant and the seeds pop. Tip the spices into the lentils, stir and taste. Adjust the seasoning if necessary, divide into 6–8 portions and freeze or chill. When you want to eat a portion, reheat it gently, wilt the spinach in the lentils, top with an egg or two, cooked the way you like it, and serve with bread and a squeeze of lemon juice to cut through the rich spices.

Variations: Try adding curry leaves, coconut milk or cream, shallots, onions, or herbs such as coriander.

Basic tomato sauce

Here's recipe that may be classified as 'basic', but believe me, it's nothing of the kind. A homemade tomato sauce is very much worth your time, and can be seasoned exactly how you like.

Makes about 6 portions

1.2kg San Marzano tomatoes
  (available fresh during
  summer, otherwise look for
  the DOP label on tins –
  you'll need 3 x 400g tins
  for this batch)
1 tbsp olive oil
3 garlic cloves, finely chopped
a pinch of fresh or dried
  oregano and/or basil
sea salt and freshly ground
  black pepper

If you're using fresh tomatoes, place them in a heatproof bowl large enough to accommodate them and pour enough boiling water over the top to cover the tomatoes. Leave them for a couple of minutes, then drain and make an incision at the top of each. Peel away the skins (or skip this step if you don't mind skin in the sauce).

Heat the oil in a large saucepan or casserole over a low-medium heat, add the garlic and cook gently for 1 minute, making sure it doesn't burn. Add the fresh or tinned tomatoes – there's no need to chop them as they'll break up during the cooking process. Stir in the oregano and/or basil, season lightly and cook for 30–45 minutes until the sauce has thickened and is a bit chunky, but not soupy. The cooking time will depend on how wide your pan is: the larger the surface area, the faster the liquid in the sauce will evaporate. Taste to check the seasoning and adjust if necessary. Transfer portions into sterilised jars while the sauce is still hot and keep them in a cool, dark place for up to a year, or freeze in containers.

Variations:
– Add a spoonful each of capers and pitted olives, and 1–2 tinned anchovy fillets (in oil) to the cooked sauce to turn it into a puttanesca sauce.
– Add red chilli flakes for a hit of spice.
– Flame-roast an aubergine (page 126), remove the skin and add the flesh to the cooked sauce.
– Add a seafood cocktail mix (or prawns) to the finished sauce to make a seafood sauce.
– Add tinned, drained beans or cooked lentils and serve it with pasta, rice and/or a salad.

Ricotta and Parmesan gnudi with sage brown butter

Akin to gnocchi, these little ricotta dumplings are a doddle to prepare – all they require is a couple of days' resting time in the fridge, then a little gentle cooking before you gobble them up (well, that's what I do because I'm greedy) with sage-infused brown butter.

250g ricotta
50g finely grated Parmesan
  cheese, plus extra to serve
  (optional)
a tiny pinch of freshly
  grated nutmeg
fine semolina, for dusting
25g butter
4 sage leaves
grated zest of ¼ unwaxed
  lemon
sea salt and freshly ground
  black pepper

Beat the ricotta and Parmesan together in a bowl. Gently season with the nutmeg (too much and the gnudi take on a slightly medicinal flavour) and a good crack of pepper. Taste the mixture before adding salt.

Scatter a layer of semolina on a tray and fill a separate bowl with semolina, to a depth of about 5cm. Using two spoons, create little spheres from the ricotta and Parmesan mixture – they don't have to be perfectly shaped – dropping each one carefully into the bowl of semolina and rolling them around so they are completely coated. Place each gnudi on the tray, leaving space between each one so they don't stick together.

Repeat until each sphere is coated, then cover the tray and refrigerate. Turn the gnudi every 12 hours or so for a couple of days – the longer you leave them the thicker the skin will be. Three days is optimal but you can cook them after two; just handle them very gently.

When you're ready to cook the gnudi, bring a saucepan of salted water to the boil. Meanwhile, heat the butter in a small pan over a high heat for 5–8 minutes until it browns and small black particles form – it should smell nutty and biscuity. Strain the brown butter through a fine-mesh sieve, coffee filter or a sieve lined with a piece of muslin or clean cloth then return the strained butter to the pan. Add the sage leaves and remove from the heat.

Carefully place the gnudi in the boiling water with a slotted spoon, making sure they don't stick to the bottom of the pan, and cook them for about 2 minutes until they rise to the surface (like gnocchi). As soon as they do this, scoop them out of the pan (you don't need to drain them in a sieve – this may result in the gnudi bursting) and serve them drizzled with the browned sage butter, with a spritz of lemon zest on top and extra Parmesan if you like.

Salads, Mezze and Tapas

—

Carrot, pomegranate and chickpea salad with a spiced citrus dressing

One of the reasons I always have a tin of chickpeas in the cupboard is so that I can make this dish. By all means use dried chickpeas if you prefer – just follow the cooking instructions on the packet and fold them into the salad once cooked and drained.

1 large carrot, washed (or peeled if you prefer) and roughly grated
1 small pomegranate, shucked
1 x 400g tin of chickpeas, drained and rinsed
small handful of toasted flaked almonds
1 banana shallot or 2 smaller shallots, peeled, finely chopped and placed in a bowl of iced water for a few minutes
1 bunch of flat-leaf parsley (or coriander), leaves finely chopped

For the spiced citrus dressing
grated zest and juice of 1 small unwaxed lemon
½ tsp ground cinnamon
½ tsp ground cumin
4–5 tbsp olive or Argan oil
sea salt and freshly ground black pepper

Place the grated carrot, pomegranate seeds, chickpeas, almonds, shallots (drained of the iced water) and parsley in a medium bowl.

Whisk the dressing ingredients together in a small bowl, season with salt and pepper and taste. If you think it needs something extra, then add it. If the dressing is too sharp, add a little sugar or honey to taste.

Dress the salad and chill it in the fridge for 1 hour or longer, to let the flavours infuse. This makes a great lunch or light supper, and can be kept for a day or so to be up-cycled into a packed lunch. Add some grilled chicken, feta, labneh, goat's cheese, mozzarella or queso fresco (or tahini and more nuts if you would like to keep it vegan).

Burrata, peaches and prosciutto with basil oil

On sultry summer days, cooking is kept to a bare minimum – this salad of soothing burrata, juicy tomatoes and ripe, sweet peaches comes alive with a vibrantly coloured basil oil and is a long-standing favourite of mine. Savoury prosciutto and a drizzle of balsamic vinegar rounds out the dish. I like to eat it freshly made as an easy supper, but you can prepare it in advance for a sumptuous packed lunch, too.

1 burrata ball
2 small, ripe doughnut peaches, or 1 ripe yellow peach, sliced into 8 pieces
1 beefsteak tomato or a mix of ripe tomatoes of choice, sliced
2–3 slices of prosciutto
handful of basil leaves
100ml olive oil
balsamic vinegar, for drizzling
freshly ground black pepper

Place the whole burrata on a dinner plate, or in a shallow pasta bowl, and scatter the peaches around it. Add the prosciutto, tearing it first or laying the slices over as they are.

Put the basil leaves in a jug or container, cover with olive oil and blitz in a small blender or with a stick blender until you have a bright green oil. Pass the oil through a sieve and drizzle a few spoonfuls of it over the salad, along with a drizzle of balsamic vinegar. A crack or two of black pepper is always welcome, but by no means mandatory.

Leftovers: You can use the remaining basil oil in a pasta dish, as a dipping oil for bread or in another salad, on another hot day. Keep it in the fridge in a sealed container until you use it again (it will keep for up to 1 week).

Antipasti skewers

In my last book, *How to Hygge*, I joked about how much I loved meat on a stick, and included a spiced, whisky chicken skewer recipe to that effect. This is a more low-fi, vegetarian version, using ingredients you can find at a deli or any good supermarket. They are perfect for those evenings when you want to curl up with a great book, and work well as a light lunch, too.

3–6 small mozzarella balls
  (depends how big they are)
3 pieces of chargrilled and
  marinated artichoke heart
3 small cherry or baby plum
  tomatoes
3 sun-blush or sun-dried
  tomatoes
6 basil leaves
6 pitted olives (3 green and
  3 black if you like)
a little drizzle of olive oil and
  balsamic vinegar (optional)

Assemble the ingredients on 3 skewers, alternating the basil leaves and olives with the other ingredients to make a pretty pattern. Drizzle a little olive oil and balsamic vinegar over them, if you wish. Eat now, or prep them for later.

Serve the skewers as they are, or with a glass of chilled white wine.

Radicchio, pink grapefruit and gorgonzola winter salad

Full of bold colours, textures and flavours, this is a super salad to try in the midwinter months when citrus fruits are at their best and you need a change from soup.

You can use dried grapefruit or orange 'crisps' (shop-bought or homemade in a low oven) instead of fresh grapefruit for an extra crunch, but juicy citrus fruits really complete this dish.

1 radicchio head
1 pink grapefruit
small wedge of gorgonzola cheese
  (I just go by eye)
small handful of toasted
  almonds
leaves from 1 sprig of thyme

For the dressing
2 tbsp olive oil
1 tbsp sherry or wine vinegar
  of choice
1 tsp wholegrain mustard
1 tsp plain or acacia honey
sea salt and freshly ground
  black pepper

Wash the radicchio and either peel the leaves all the way off or give the head a rough chop. Place the leaves in a shallow pasta bowl or on a dinner plate, then peel the grapefruit, and slice the flesh (thickly enough that the slices hold their shape) and scatter it on top. Place little bites of gorgonzola around the salad. Scatter over the almonds and thyme leaves.

Mix the dressing ingredients together in a jam jar or cup (if using a jam jar, just seal and give it a really good shake to emulsify the vinaigrette) and taste. I like a very punchy, vinegar-rich dressing for this salad but if you prefer a more traditional vinaigrette, simply add a spoonful or two more olive oil until you have the consistency and flavour you like.

Drizzle the dressing on top of the salad and keep any spare for dunking bread into.

Variations:
– Radicchio also marries well with pear and apple and, if you're a fan of bitter flavours, blood orange.
– Use other leaves such as chicory, frisée, watercress or rocket, if you prefer.
– Lightly grill the radicchio if you fancy a warmer salad: chop it and lace it with a little oil then grill or quickly pan-fry it.

Green gazpacho

Gazpacho is the perfect refresher on a hot summer's day or evening. Given how many greens are in this version I like to think of it as a savoury form of Berocca: just the shot of natural vitamins you need when you're flagging from the heat…

1 green bell pepper, halved
  and deseeded
¼ cucumber, roughly chopped
4–5 tbsp olive oil
1 small bunch of coriander,
  leaves and stems
1 small bunch of flat-leaf
  parsley, leaves and stems
1 green tomato, roughly
  chopped
1 spring onion or shallot,
  roughly chopped
1 fat slice of stale white bread or
  sourdough, roughly chopped
1 garlic clove, peeled
1 tbsp vinegar (white wine,
  cider or sherry vinegar all
  work well)
sea salt and freshly ground
  black pepper
extra cucumber, finely
  chopped, to garnish
1 fresh green chilli, deseeded and
  finely chopped, to garnish (leave
  the seeds in if you want it spicy)
ice cubes

Place all the ingredients (except the salt and pepper, garnish and ice cubes) in a blender or food processor and blitz until smooth. I like to keep some texture to it but some prefer a very smooth gazpacho, in which case pass it through a sieve. Season to taste. Bear in mind that this soup is eaten very cold (with ice cubes) so the flavour will be slightly muted by refrigeration. In other words, don't be shy about seasoning generously. After all, if you're in the midst of a heatwave you'll be sweating intensely, so you'll need to consume some salt to recalibrate.

Chill the soup for 1–2 hours in the fridge, or place in the freezer for 30 minutes–1 hour until very cold. Serve with ice cubes, garnished with finely chopped cucumber and green chilli.

Note: You can divide this in half and have a cup alongside another dish, or with tapas (pages 121–25) and Pan con Tomate (page 29), and save the second cup for lunch the next day.

Canarian salt-wrinkled potatoes with mojo verde

These little wrinkly potatoes make a terrific *tapa*, or snack, alongside some Spanish Manzanilla olives, vinegar-soused anchovies and Garlic Prawns (page 123), but you can spin the spuds into a simple meal by serving them alongside a green salad and a couple of fried eggs. They also match well with seafood such as grilled fish, or the Roasted Sea Bass (page 38).

500ml water
50g sea salt
150g small salad potatoes, Jersey Royals or Anyas

For the mojo verde
1 bunch of coriander leaves
1 fresh green chilli
1 garlic clove, crushed
1 tsp ground cumin
4 tbsp olive oil
1–2 tbsp sherry vinegar (or other vinegar of choice)
½ tsp pimenton dulce (or picante if you like it hot)
sea salt and freshly ground black pepper

Bring the water to the boil in a pan with the sea salt then add the baby potatoes to the salted water. Cook for 30 minutes, then drain. Return the potatoes to the pan and let them steam-dry, over a very low heat if you wish, then cover the pan with a cloth (off the heat) so they wrinkle slightly.

Serve the potatoes warm or at room temperature with the mojo verde. The mojo verde can be made in advance but can also be eaten immediately: mix all the ingredients together in a blender or food processor and pulse a few times. I like quite a rough-textured mojo verde but if you prefer a smooth sauce keep blending until you have the consistency you like. Add more olive oil if needed, and a little water if it's too dry. Season to taste.

Tabbouleh

Light and aromatic, this green herb and lemony salad from the
Middle East makes a great packed lunch or modest supper.

1 tbsp fine bulgur wheat

4 ripe cherry or baby plum
   tomatoes, finely chopped

¼ cucumber, deseeded and
   finely chopped

grated zest and juice of
   ½ unwaxed lemon

a pinch of ground cinnamon

a pinch of ground coriander

1 small bunch of parsley,
   leaves very finely chopped

½ small bunch of mint,
   leaves very finely chopped

1 spring onion, thinly sliced

2 tbsp olive oil

sea salt and freshly ground
   black pepper

1 small baby gem lettuce,
   to serve

grilled halloumi and flatbread
   or pita bread, to serve (optional)

First, soak the bulgur wheat according to
the packet instructions. Drain it well so
it's not soggy when you make the salad.
Place it in a medium bowl and add the
chopped tomatoes, cucumber, lemon
zest and juice, and the spices, and mix
well with a spoon.

Fold in the herbs and spring onion, then
drizzle over the olive oil. Taste and season
with salt and pepper accordingly. If you
think it needs more lemon juice, spices or
olive oil, go for it. This is a salad that you
can make your own, so taste as you go.

Cover and set aside for 1 hour, or up to
a few hours, before serving with baby gem
lettuce leaves and flatbread or pita bread
if you wish.

Variations:
*– Some people like to add a finely crushed
garlic clove to tabbouleh, others like to add
a little heat in the form of chilli pepper.*
*– If you can't source bulgur wheat, couscous
works, too. Couscous (and garlic/chilli) may
not be traditional tabbouleh ingredients,
strictly speaking, but purists will always
gripe about something. Do what seems
right to you, using ingredients you can
readily source.*

Garlic prawns (*Gambas al ajillo*)

Having tried many iterations of prawns in garlic over the years I found a lot of recipes were quite flat in flavour, but more frustratingly, the garlic was incinerated and acrid in taste from being overcooked. So, when I came across a clever way to intensify both the garlic flavour and the prawn flavour from J. Kenji López-Alt on Serious Eats I had to give it a go. Mine's a slightly simplified version, and can be adapted using other spices and herbs.

4 small garlic cloves
8 raw prawns, peeled with
   their tails intact (reserve
   the shells)
olive oil
1 sprig of flat-leaf parsley,
   leaves roughly chopped
   (reserve the stalk)
1 small, dried chilli or a
   sprinkle of red chilli flakes
   (optional)
sea salt flakes (or crunchy
   rock salt if you prefer)
a slice of bread, to serve
   (optional)

Finely chop 1 garlic clove (or grate it – a Microplane grater works well if you have one). Put the raw prawns in a small bowl and coat them in the garlic.

Roughly crush another garlic clove and place it in a small saucepan or frying pan with enough oil to fill the pan to a depth of 1cm. Put the pan over a low-medium heat, add the prawn shells, parsley stalk and chilli (if using) and infuse the oil with the flavourings for 5–8 minutes. Keep an eye on the oil – the shells should turn coral-pink and the garlic should take on a golden colour (but don't let it burn). When the oil is aromatic, carefully give the shells a little crush so they release all their flavour before using a slotted spoon or a small sieve to fish out the shells, garlic, parsley stalk and chilli. Discard all of the flavourings (or keep them to snack on if that's your thing).

Thinly slice the 2 remaining garlic cloves. Sprinkle a little salt on the prawns and increase the heat under the pan to medium-high. Add the prawns (they should sizzle when you add them to the oil) and the sliced garlic and cook until the prawns just turn opaque and light pink in colour – up to 1 minute on each side – and remove immediately (remove the garlic, too). Serve scattered with the chopped parsley, an extra sprinkle of salt and eat hot. I reckon a slice of bread is essential for mopping up all the garlicky, prawn-y juices but you can eat this dish on its own, too.

Tzatziki

This works well as a mezze dip for cosy nights in or as an easy sauce to accompany grilled fish, meat and vegetables. In Scandinavia we often refer to dill as the 'garlic of the North' – this tzatziki recipe forgoes mint in favour of the more pungent dill. If you prefer other herbs then feel free to mix it up. (Pictured on pages 128–9.)

½ cucumber, halved
  lengthways and deseeded
  (skin on)
1 garlic clove, finely chopped
2 tbsp olive oil
250g Greek yoghurt
1 tsp white wine or
  cider vinegar
1 bunch of dill, finely
  chopped
sea salt and freshly ground
  black pepper

Roughly grate the cucumber and put it in a sieve. Set the sieve over a bowl or suspend it over the kitchen sink, and sprinkle 1 teaspoon of salt over the top, mixing it into the cucumber. Leave it for about 15 minutes, pressing down on the cucumber a few times with the back of a spoon to help release excess liquid.

In a separate bowl, combine the garlic and olive oil, then mix in the Greek yoghurt and vinegar. Add the chopped dill and stir well.

After one final squeeze to get rid of any remaining liquid, pat the cucumber dry with kitchen paper, then fold it into the yoghurt mixture. It should be quite thick. Season to taste with salt and pepper (and extra vinegar, if needed) and chill in the fridge until you're ready to eat it.

Artichoke, almond and Parmesan dip

As an artichoke obsessive I always have a jar of chargrilled 'chokes in my kitchen cupboard, either to snack on, to jazz up a simple salad or to make this full-flavoured dip.

Think of this as a pale tapenade – minus the black olives. You can enjoy it in myriad ways: paired with crispbread, pita bread, tortilla chips, or with a rainbow of crudités – radish, carrot, cucumber and pepper work especially well.

175g chargrilled jarred
  artichokes
4 tbsp grated Parmesan cheese
grated zest and juice of
  ½ unwaxed lemon
4–5 tbsp olive oil
handful of toasted almonds
sea salt and freshly ground
  black pepper

Put all the ingredients (except the salt and pepper) in a blender or food processor and blitz until quite smooth and evenly combined. You can make it in a pestle and mortar too, but you'll need to finely chop the artichokes first, then crush all the ingredients with the pestle, crushing the nuts first before adding the cheese, lemon and oil, followed by the chopped artichokes. This will give the dip a rougher texture, but it will be no less delicious for it.

Season the dip with salt and pepper to taste, eat fresh and keep whatever is left over in a covered container in the fridge for up to a week. When I've tired of using it as a dip, I spread it on sourdough toast a few days after making it and scatter rocket leaves, ripe sliced tomatoes (or sun-blush/dried tomatoes) and olives on top. Any greenery really complements this dip, and if you've made the Grilled Citrus, Chilli and Vegetable Medley on page 72 try adding them, too.

Baba ganoush

An intensely smoky baba ganoush is well worth making from scratch –
an open flame (either the gas hob or a barbecue grill) really brings out
that smoky flavour, but you can also use an oven grill or very hot oven.
(Pictured on pages 128–9.)

1 large aubergine
1 small garlic clove, finely
  chopped
2 tbsp olive oil, plus extra
  for drizzling
2 tbsp tahini
1 sprig of mint, leaves shredded
1 sprig of flat-leaf parsley,
  leaves shredded
juice of ½ unwaxed lemon
  (you can grate in some of the
  zest, too)
a pinch of chilli powder
  (optional)
a pinch of ground cumin,
  gently toasted (optional)
sea salt

Line your hob surface with foil to catch
any drips from the grilled aubergine as it
cooks. Place the whole aubergine directly
over a low gas hob flame and keep turning
it every few minutes. It will spit, hiss, smoke
and start to shrivel after about 20 minutes.
Hold your nerve and keep it on the flame
for around 30 minutes, so the smoky
flavour from the skin permeates all the flesh
and the aubergine loses its 'sponginess'.

Once the aubergine has collapsed into a
slippery, smoky mess, turn off the heat and
transfer the aubergine to a chopping board.
Leave it to cool for a few minutes then peel
off the skin, trying to keep as much of the
flesh as possible (scraping off some of it
that's stuck to the skin as you peel it off).
Put the aubergine flesh in a sieve over a bowl
or the kitchen sink and leave it to drain for
30 minutes, adding a spoonful of sea salt to
help drive off the excess liquid.

Meanwhile, mix all the remaining
ingredients together in a bowl.

Add the drained aubergine to the rest of
the ingredients, folding everything together
so you have a silky baba ganoush.

Season to taste with more salt (and tweak
with more herbs, tahini, garlic or lemon,
if you wish), drizzle a little extra olive oil
on top and eat immediately. Whatever you
don't polish off can be kept in an airtight
container in the fridge for up to a week.

Heritage tomato, pomegranate molasses and oregano salad

Obviously, there are countless ways to prepare a tomato salad. I tend to save this version for the spring/summer months when a rainbow of heritage tomatoes are available, but you can make it with whatever tomatoes you find. It's a dish that can be enjoyed on its own, or accompanied by pita bread, and you can add feta, halloumi (or whatever cheese you favour) into the mix for extra nourishment… (Pictured overleaf.)

an assortment of yellow, red,
 green and orange heritage
 tomatoes (they vary in size, but
 about 4–5 medium ones)
1 shallot, thinly sliced and
 placed in a bowl of iced
 water for a few minutes
5–6 walnuts
leaves from 3 sprigs of oregano
pomegranate molasses,
 for drizzling
sea salt and freshly ground
 black pepper

Slice the tomatoes to your desired thickness and place them in a bowl or on a dinner plate. Scatter the shallot (drained of its iced water) and walnuts on top, along with the oregano leaves. Drizzle pomegranate molasses over everything and season with a little salt and pepper before serving.

Simple
Pleasures

—

Nasu dengaku
(Japanese miso grilled aubergine)

The humble aubergine is a solo cook's friend: I love how its texture transforms from spongy to meltingly tender when you apply heat. A dish I often turn to when I crave something vegetarian, *nasu dengaku* is also a fitting accompaniment to grilled fish, a crisp salad, sticky rice and some Japanese pickles.

1 medium aubergine
vegetable or sunflower oil,
  for frying
toasted sesame seeds,
  to garnish

For the miso marinade
2 tsp red miso paste (for a
  milder, sweeter version use
  shiro or white miso paste)
1–2 tsp soft light brown sugar
1–2 tsp mirin, light vinegar
  such as white wine or cider
  vinegar or lemon juice
1 tbsp toasted sesame oil

Start by slicing the aubergine in half lengthways and carefully make shallow cuts in a criss-cross diamond pattern in the flesh of both halves. Brush the cut sides of the aubergine halves with a little oil.

Place a skillet or frying pan over a medium heat, add the aubergine halves cut-side down and cook for a few minutes until the cut sides start to brown, then turn them over and cook for a few more minutes skin-side down until completely soft. Liquid will start to come out of the aubergine into the pan – that's a good sign.

Preheat the grill to medium.

Mix together the ingredients for the miso marinade in a bowl and taste it. It should have a delicious savoury flavour – add more miso, brown sugar, vinegar and/or sesame oil as you see fit. Remember, the aubergine is quite bland so you want the marinade to have a really punchy flavour.

Put the aubergine halves on a grill tray cut-side up. Brush half the marinade over each aubergine, on the cut side, and grill for a few minutes until the miso marinade sizzles and caramelises slightly. Remove from the grill and scatter sesame seeds on top. Eat while warm.

Chilled Japanese soba noodles with cucumber and a sesame and miso dressing

If you've never tried chilled soba noodles you're in for a treat. I learnt how to make this dish when I spent time in Japan before I went to university. Japanese summers are famously hot and sticky, so this chilled dish has an immediately restorative effect when you're wilting from the heat.

100g soba noodles (100% buckwheat are best for this)
⅓ cucumber, cut into ribbons with a vegetable peeler or into small cubes for a contrast with the soba
2 spring onions, thinly sliced
ice cubes, for chilling the noodles

For the dressing
1 tbsp toasted sesame oil
1 tbsp mirin (mirin is traditional but you can use white wine or cider vinegar)
1 tsp red miso paste
1 tsp soft light brown sugar or palm sugar
½ tsp soy sauce or kombu sauce

Optional extra garnishes
black and/or white sesame seeds
wasabi paste
Japanese pickles
sprouted greens (alfalfa, broccoli, cress or radish all work well)
shiso leaves, shredded
grated fresh root ginger

Cook the noodles according to the packet instructions until al dente (usually about 5 minutes) then immediately drain and chill in a sieve with a few ice cubes.

Whisk the ingredients for the dressing together in a small bowl and taste. It should have quite a savoury-sour flavour. If necessary, add more vinegar, miso paste or sesame oil until it tastes the way you like it.

Ditch the ice cubes and place the chilled noodles in a shallow pasta bowl or plate along with the cucumber and spring onion. Add any of the garnishes that appeal to you and drizzle the dressing over the cold noodles. Quench your third with a tall glass of iced green or oolong tea alongside.

Asparagus, Parmesan and pancetta

Come late spring and early summer British asparagus is bountiful.
I find myself picking up a bunch at least a couple of times a week
to make the most of the short season.

1 small pack of diced smoked
  pancetta (about 75g)
1 medium bunch of asparagus
  spears, washed and tough
  ends snapped off
Parmesan cheese, to taste
sea salt and freshly ground
  black pepper
extra-virgin or regular olive oil,
  for drizzling (optional)

Start by frying the pancetta in a pan. If it's
quite fatty you won't need any oil but if
it's lean add a spoonful of oil to the pan to
stop it from sticking. Cook until golden brown
and the fat has rendered so it's quite crispy.

Remove the pancetta from the pan and set
it aside for a moment. Place the asparagus
spears in the same pan along with a little
water, some salt and a sprinkle of pepper.
Cover with a lid and cook over a medium heat
for a few minutes until steam rises and they
start caramelising: really fat asparagus spears
will need 3–4 minutes, thinner ones will only
need around 2 minutes to cook through.

Arrange the asparagus spears on a plate,
top with the pancetta and shave as much
Parmesan as you like over the top. Drizzle
with olive oil if you wish and eat while warm.

Variations:
– Use pecorino instead of Parmesan, or try
it with some Gorwydd Caerphilly or Mrs
Kirkham's Lancashire cheese.
– If you wish to add some heat, try frying
a chopped red or green chilli alongside the
pancetta, or sprinkle some chilli flakes on
top of the finished dish.
– If you like a melted cheese effect you can
grill the cheese briefly, although do this on
a heatproof tray or tin before transferring
the cheesy asparagus on to a plate.

Fish finger sandwich with Nordic dill salsa

Here's a strong contender for my favourite semi-cheat meal ever. Admittedly a good old fish finger sarnie tastes incredible with just a good squirt of ketchup, but once in a while I like a fresh green sauce to grace those crispy little fish sticks. This dill salsa is a great way of using up any odds and ends you have in the fridge – such as sad, forgotten herbs, condiments and pickles. Treat the recipe as a guide and please do play around with the flavours to make it your own.

4 frozen fish fingers
2 slices of bread of your choice
butter, for spreading (and
 frying, if you wish)

For the dill salsa
small bunch of dill
small bunch of parsley
2 tinned anchovies (Abba
 are best for this, but you can
 use Spanish or Italian)
3 small gherkins (the more
 sour the better)
1 tsp capers, rinsed
grated zest and juice of
 1 small unwaxed lemon
2–3 tbsp olive oil
1 tsp horseradish sauce

Start by making the dill salsa. Put all the ingredients in a blender or food processor and blitz until quite evenly blended, or chop them up and crush them together in a pestle and mortar, adding more lemon juice to loosen it, or oil or water if you prefer.

Cook the fish fingers according to the packet instructions, and while they're cooking, lightly toast or grill the bread. If you've had a really rotten day, or spent it doing seriously strenuous exercise, fry the bread in butter.

Spread the toast with butter, place the cooked fish fingers on top of one slice and drizzle with the dill salsa. Top with the other slice of bread.

Leftovers: Cover any leftover salsa and store it in the fridge to use for dressing salads, beans, other seafood or freshly cooked new potatoes. You can also use it in other sandwiches; the flavours pair well with roasted ham, smoked chicken, pastrami and any number of deli-style cured meats.

Lemon, courgette and ricotta fritters

Some days you want pancakes for dinner, but then you remember you also need to eat your daily greens. This is a compromise of sorts, but by no means a fudge – you get lots of flavour from the Parmesan and it's a nifty way to use up courgette, in all honesty a vegetable I'm not overly enamoured with. You can always add a few extra greens on the side too: tenderstem broccoli, a fennel salad or leftover roast vegetables from page 72 pair well with this dish.

1 small courgette, roughly
  grated
100g ricotta
3 tbsp grated Parmesan
  cheese
1 egg
3 tbsp self-raising white flour
  (or wholemeal if you prefer)
grated zest and juice of
  ½ unwaxed lemon
vegetable or sunflower oil,
  for frying
sea salt and freshly ground
  black pepper
salad of rocket, toasted flaked
  almonds and sliced tomatoes,
  to serve
spoonful of Basic Tomato Sauce
  (page 103), to serve (optional)

Stir all the ingredients (except the oil, salt and pepper) together in a bowl until you have a thick batter.

Pour oil into a saucepan to a depth of about 2.5cm and place over a medium heat. If you drop a small piece of bread into the oil it should crisp up within 30 seconds (if you have a thermometer, the oil should be 160°C).

Using an ice-cream scoop or a tablespoon, scoop a heaped spoonful of mixture into the hot oil (just one at first, to test the batter for consistency and seasoning). Fry it for a minute or so until golden brown, turning it over with a slotted spoon to make sure it fries evenly, then scoop it out with a slotted spoon and drain on kitchen paper, leaving it to cool for a few moments. Taste this first fritter: you may need to add more salt and pepper to the batter, or an extra spoonful of flour to help the fritters hold together. Continue with the rest of the batter, frying 3 fritters at a time for a few minutes until they look golden brown and are cooked through. Drain on kitchen paper.

Serve warm, with the salad on the side, and the tomato sauce if you want to make it more substantial.

Scallops and sherry

Forget fiddling around with a messy lobster. To my mind, a plate of perfectly cooked scallops is one of the most delicious, indulgent treats a solo cook can make for her, or himself.

5 scallops, roe intact (or remove it if you prefer)
1 banana shallot or 2–3 smaller shallots, finely chopped
1 garlic clove, finely chopped
50ml fino or Manzanilla sherry
1 sprig of tarragon, flat-leaf parsley, chives or dill, finely chopped
1 tbsp cold butter, cut into small cubes, plus 1 tsp
sea salt and freshly ground black pepper
crusty bread, to serve

Preheat the oven to 160°C/gas mark 2.

Dry the scallops well on kitchen paper and season them with salt and pepper.

Melt the teaspoon of butter in a skillet or frying pan over a medium-high heat and as soon as it's foaming, add the scallops. Fry them for 1–2 minutes on each side – each side should develop a caramelised crust. Don't overcook them as they're going in the oven next. Transfer the scallops to a small baking tray or roasting dish and put them in the oven.

While the scallops are in the oven, add the shallot to the same skillet or frying pan and fry for a couple of minutes, then add the garlic and cook a further 30 seconds. Add the sherry, boil vigorously and reduce by about a third, then add the chopped herbs and whisk in each cold cube of butter so you have an emulsified sauce. Remove the scallops from the oven, taste the sauce for seasoning and adjust if necessary before serving the scallops with the sauce drizzled all round, along with the bread to mop up the sauce.

Eat while warm, with a glass of chilled sherry alongside.

Variations:
– Instead of sherry you can use vermouth, or a generous spoonful of flambéed brandy along with a spritz of lemon juice.
– Add some double cream or crème fraîche instead of the cubed, cold butter if you prefer a creamier sauce.

Salade Niçoise

As an anchovy fiend, I prefer this version of the classic Niçoise salad, but please do go ahead and replace the anchovies with tuna (tinned or freshly grilled) or, for an oilier fish hit, sardines (again, tinned or grilled), if anchovies aren't to your taste.

handful of French green
   beans, blanched and
   refreshed in iced water
1 small shallot, thinly sliced
   and placed in a bowl of iced
   water for a few minutes,
   then drained
2 ripe, fat tomatoes, thickly sliced
¼ cucumber, roughly chopped
4 radishes, quartered or
   sliced into slivers
1 egg, hard-boiled, peeled
   and quartered
1 tsp capers, rinsed
3 tinned anchovy fillets,
   sliced into slivers
small handful of basil leaves
   (optional)
a few olives of choice
sea salt and freshly ground
   black pepper

For the vinaigrette
1 tsp wholegrain mustard
grated zest and juice of ½ small
   unwaxed lemon
2 tbsp olive oil

Start by making the vinaigrette: stir the mustard, lemon zest and juice together in a bowl. Whisk in the olive oil gradually so the vinaigrette emulsifies. If you can't be bothered, simply place the ingredients in a small jam jar, cover with the lid and give it a really good shake. Season to taste with salt and pepper (bearing in mind that the anchovies will be salty).

On a plate or in a wide, shallow pasta bowl assemble all the remaining ingredients. Drizzle the vinaigrette over the top and eat.

Variations:
– Try using blanched broad beans or asparagus instead of the beans.
– If you like raw pepper, add some chopped red or yellow pepper to the salad.
– Give the salad some extra heft with a small sliced or chopped avocado.

Leftovers: If you have more radishes than you need, do as the French do and eat them with cold, unsalted butter and a sprinkle of sea salt as a delightful snack.

Nutty, tahini-laced dates

My friend Dana Elemara, food entrepreneur and founder of Arganic, is one of the most wonderful people I've met in a decade working in the food business, and she kindly gave me this idea.

I won't claim they're 'healthy' as such, but these tahini-laced dates are a great alternative for those days when you feel you may have hit the butter shortbread a little too hard of late yet need to satisfy a sweet tooth.

Think of them as little bursts of energy to be consumed in moderation, preferably before you're about to do some form of exercise. Pack them into a little Tupperware box and take them on long walks to sustain you. A cup of unsweetened tea or coffee alongside these dates will power you through whatever activity you choose to embark on.

3 plump dates, stones
  removed
3 tsp tahini paste
a sprinkle of green, raw
  pistachios (Iranian or Turkish
  are best), crushed, or
  pistachio nibs

Turn each date over so the slit where the stone was faces upwards. Spoon the tahini paste into each date and sprinkle the pistachios on top.

Variations:
– If you're a chocoholic like I am, melt some dark chocolate (70% cocoa solids, or higher if you like a stronger flavour) and either drizzle the melted chocolate over the dates or dip each date into the chocolate to create a mock truffle.
– Different ingredients that work well scattered on top of the stuffed dates include desiccated coconut, other nuts such as almonds, walnuts and pecans and – if you have a freshly shucked pomegranate – pomegranate seeds.

Note: Scale up the quantities of this snack to make larger amounts to keep for the week ahead.

Roast portobello mushroom with garlic, blue cheese and hazelnuts

The secret to a perfect mushroom is to cook it thoroughly, so much so that it releases all its excess liquid and really concentrates in flavour. You want the portobello mushroom quite shriveled for this dish to really work.

2 tsp lightly salted butter
1 large portobello mushroom, brushed or wiped clean, and stem removed (keep for cooking)
1 tsp vegetable or sunflower oil
1 banana shallot, finely chopped
1 small garlic clove, finely chopped
1 fresh green chilli, finely chopped
leaves from 1 sprig of thyme (or a few chives, finely chopped)
2 tbsp breadcrumbs
1 tbsp crushed hazelnuts
30g blue cheese of choice, broken into chunks
sea salt and freshly ground black pepper

Preheat the oven to 220°C/gas mark 7.

Melt the butter in a small saucepan, skillet or frying pan, then brush the mushroom on both sides with the melted butter. Season with a little salt and pepper, place the mushroom in a small roasting dish and cook in the oven for about 10 minutes until the mushroom releases a lot of its liquid and shrivels to two-thirds of its original size.

While the mushroom is in the oven, add the oil to the remaining butter in the saucepan or frying pan, place over a medium heat, add the shallot and cook for 3–5 minutes or until it is translucent, then add the garlic. Cook for a further 30 seconds to release the flavour of the garlic, until it turns translucent too. Add the thyme leaves (or chives) and stir again. Add the breadcrumbs and hazelnuts, season with salt and pepper, then spoon the mixture into the middle of the roasted mushroom and top with the blue cheese.

Place the dish back in the oven or under a preheated grill for a couple of minutes, until the cheese melts. If you like it golden and with a little crispness, keep it in the oven or under the grill for a few minutes longer. Remove and eat the mushroom warm, on toast or with a salad of choice.

Lazy
Weekends

Kimchi pancakes

Fiery, savoury pancakes may not be that common in the UK but by golly they deserve to be. I love the manifold flavours of this dish, adapted from a recipe by my friend Judy Joo, the brilliant Korean-American chef, broadcaster and food writer. These pancakes are so easy to rustle up and make an excellent brunch on a cold winter's weekend, or a simple supper during a dark evening.

For the dipping sauce
2 tbsp soy sauce
1 tbsp mirin (or white wine
  vinegar)
1 tbsp toasted sesame oil
1 tbsp toasted sesame seeds
1 tsp soft light brown sugar
1 tsp Korean or Aleppo chilli
  flakes (or 1 green chilli,
  finely chopped)
1 spring onion, thinly sliced
  on the diagonal
sea salt and freshly ground
  black pepper

For the pancake batter
150g kimchi, drained and roughly
  chopped (plus 2 tbsp of the liquid)
60g rice flour
2 tbsp plain flour
2 spring onions, thinly sliced
1 egg
1 tsp soft light brown sugar
1 garlic clove, finely grated
  or chopped
a pinch of sea salt
vegetable or sunflower oil,
  for frying

Combine all the dipping sauce ingredients in a bowl. Season to taste with salt and pepper and set aside while you prepare the pancake batter.

Mix all the batter ingredients (except the oil) together in a medium bowl until you have a thick, lumpy batter.

Heat 2 tablespoons of oil in a skillet, frying pan or crêpe pan over a medium heat and pour in a little of the batter to make 2 pancakes. Fry the pancakes for 2–3 minutes, then flip them over to cook for 2–3 minutes on the other side. Remove from the pan and continue with the remaining batter: you should get 6 in total, depending on their size and the size of your pan.

Serve the warm pancakes with the dipping sauce.

Sugar plum French toast

The season of mellow fruitfulness is cause for celebration every year: long walks in the woods when the leaves change from green to gold, cooler evenings for a better night's sleep and autumn's bounty of ingredients to savour... this dish is a prime example of what to do when British plums arrive.

The amount of plums here may seem like a lot, but it's worth roasting a larger batch as leftovers are delicious the next day in porridge, on Greek yoghurt, with buttered toast or on fluffy American-style pancakes (overleaf).

1 egg
50ml whole milk
1 tbsp soft light brown sugar
½ tsp vanilla extract
¼ tsp sea salt
2 large slices of stale sourdough
  bread, country loaf or brioche
1 tsp butter

For the roast plums
10 red plums (roughly
  1 punnet), halved and stoned
15g butter, melted
2 tbsp soft light brown sugar

To serve (any combination
of the following)
maple syrup
ground cinnamon
crème fraîche or Greek yoghurt
blackberries

Preheat the oven to 200°C/gas mark 6 and line a roasting dish or baking tin with baking parchment.

Place the halved plums cut-side up on the parchment and brush them with a little melted butter. Sprinkle the sugar on top – if they're sour, hard plums you may need to use more sugar. Bake for 15 minutes, or until the plums are soft. Remove from the oven and set aside while you prepare the French toast.

Crack the egg into a shallow dish or bowl wide enough to fit the slices of bread (halve the bread slices if need be) and use a fork to mix in the milk, sugar, vanilla and salt. Soak the bread in the mixture for 1–2 minutes, turning each slice over so they get evenly soaked. Melt the butter in a frying pan over a medium heat until foaming and place the eggy bread in the pan. Turn down the heat to medium-low and fry for 1–2 minutes, or until the bread is golden and crisp underneath, then turn the slices over and fry on the other side.

Place the French toast on kitchen paper to absorb excess fat, then plate up with the roasted plums and any other toppings your heart desires (I like a lot of maple syrup!).

Variation: Add alcohol to the plums before you roast them – a splash of sherry, brandy, Marsala wine or Madeira all work well.

Fluffy, American-style buttermilk pancakes

Adding buttermilk to this pancake recipe really helps fluff up the batter when cooking, and you can make these sweet or savoury, or both! For a true American breakfast top them with blueberries, maple syrup and crispy bacon.

Makes 4–6 pancakes

125g plain flour
½ tsp bicarbonate of soda
2 tsp caster sugar
¼ tsp fine sea salt
180ml buttermilk (or whole milk acidulated with a little lemon juice or vinegar)
25g butter, melted, plus extra for frying and to serve (optional)
1 egg, lightly beaten
½ tsp vanilla extract

Toppings
fresh berries, chopped banana, spices such as cinnamon and cardamom, compote, honey, maple syrup, cooked bacon, Greek yoghurt, ricotta, ice cream, chocolate sauce, salted caramel... you name it: whatever you need to top these pancakes with, go for it.

Preheat the oven to 120°C/gas mark ½ and put a clean oven tray or wire rack in the middle of the oven.

Sift the flour and bicarbonate of soda into a bowl, then stir in the sugar and salt. Make a well in the middle and add the buttermilk, melted butter, egg and vanilla. Stir until you have a thick batter – it shouldn't be runny like crêpes, more like a sludgy, starchy, moveable mass.

Melt 1 teaspoon of butter in a skillet, flat frying pan or crêpe pan over a medium heat. Once it's slightly sizzling, spoon in a ladleful of pancake batter and turn down the heat to low-medium. Cook for a minute or two until the pancake is golden brown and crisp on the base, then flip it over with a spatula or palette knife and fry for another minute or so, until evenly cooked. The inside might look a little undercooked, but don't worry – they'll keep cooking in the warm oven.

Place the pancake in the oven, on the tray or wire rack, and repeat with the rest of the batter.

Serve them hot with toppings of choice, and extra butter if you like.

Variations:
– Add a mashed banana to the batter.
– Add blueberries or chocolate chips to the batter.

Leftovers: Separate cooked pancakes with sheets of greaseproof paper and freeze. Reheat in a warm oven for a few minutes to revive them.

The full Irish

With its rich food culture and seemingly limitless hospitality, I have a real soft spot for the Emerald Isle. From Dublin to Waterford, Cork and all the way over to Kerry, I've always eaten well and met great people – and of course, much like their British neighbours, they understand the value of a good breakfast. This dish is the perfect lazy weekend treat to set you up for whatever lies ahead.

butter
150g small waxy potatoes, sliced into discs the thickness of a £1 coin
1 small Irish white pudding, sliced into 1cm-thick discs
5 button or chestnut mushrooms, cleaned and halved, and lightly oiled or brushed with melted butter
2 eggs
1–2 slices of Sprouted Multigrain Soda Bread (page 98)
sea salt and freshly ground black pepper

Preheat the oven to 180°C/gas mark 4.

Lightly grease a medium roasting tray or ovenproof skillet with butter and cover the bottom with the discs of potato, then top with the white pudding and mushrooms and season with a little salt and a good crack of pepper.

Roast in the oven for 30–40 minutes, or until the spuds are tender and golden brown, and both the white pudding and mushrooms have browned at the edges and taken on a good colour.

Remove the tray or skillet from the oven and nudge some of the ingredients to create two shallow dents. Crack an egg into each dent and put the tray or skillet back in the oven. Bake for a further 5 minutes, or until the eggs are cooked to your liking.

Remove from the oven, eat hot from the pan along with a slice or two of buttered soda bread and a cup of Barry's Tea.

Variations:
– Add a few tomatoes to the potato and white pudding mix if you wish.
– Black pudding or Irish sausage can be substituted for the white pudding.

Solo breakfast

A solo breakfast on the weekend is one of the finest rituals – honestly, it's the meal I look forward to more than any other and in our hectic, digitally wired times it's also an essential way to recalibrate.

Switch off all screens for an hour or so, put on the radio, a record player or Spotify and really savour this time to yourself. Make the effort to decorate your breakfast table or bench with a small posy of flowers, or a plant, and light a candle if it's dark and miserable outside. Place a napkin next to your plate. Whatever makes you feel content as you sit down to eat, do it with relish. (Pictured overleaf.)

a pot of tea (green or black)
a glass of kefir or similar
  drinking yoghurt
1 or 2 eggs, at room temperature
½ pink or ruby grapefruit, sliced
  into wedges
a little pot of Peach Freezer Jam
  (page 94)
porridge or Vanilla Overnight Oats
  (page 95)
1 or 2 slices of sourdough or
  wholemeal bread, or a slice of
  Sprouted Multigrain Soda Bread
  (page 98)
butter, for spreading
honey
sea salt and freshly ground
  black pepper

Start by setting the table and preparing the tea, drinking yoghurt and any condiments and seasonings you wish to grace your breakfast with.

Have whatever reading material you require to hand, or turn the radio on so you can sit down and properly savour everything.

Bring a small saucepan of water to the boil then turn the heat down to a simmer and add the egg(s). For a soft-boiled egg, simmer for 5 minutes, or 6 minutes (or longer) if you prefer a harder-set yolk. Remove the pan from the heat, drain and run the eggs under cold water in the sink so they don't overcook. Place them in egg cups on the table, along with the grapefruit and Freezer Jam and porridge.

Toast the bread and butter it. Sit down to eat and repeat this ritual every weekend, or whenever you need a restorative hour to start your day.

Variations:
– Tabasco adds a great kick to a soft-boiled egg.
– Abba anchovies are a Johansen-family favourite for spreading on buttered toast, before dunking in that yolk.
– Herrings or smoked salmon add a Scandi touch. As we Norwegians say, make it as koselig or hyggelig as possible…

Chorizo and jalapeño quesadilla

A buttery, crisp quesadilla wrap with smoky chorizo, spicy jalapeño pepper and lots of oozing cheese. What's not to love?

½ tsp butter
1 flour tortilla or flatbread wrap
1 small handful (around
   4 tbsp) roughly grated
   mozzarella/Cheddar/Monterey
   Jack (or whichever melting
   cheese mix you prefer)
6 thin, deli-style slices of
   chorizo (i.e. not the plump
   cooking sausages)
2 tbsp sliced pickled jalapeño
   peppers (from a jar) (or more/
   less depending on your
   preference for heat/spice)
1 small bunch of coriander, leaves
   roughly chopped, and some
   stems finely chopped, plus
   extra to serve (optional)
1 spring onion, thinly sliced
½ lime (optional)
Tabasco, to taste
sea salt and freshly ground
   black pepper

Rub a skillet or frying pan with the butter in an even layer and place it over a medium heat.

Pop the tortilla wrap in the pan and scatter an even layer of grated cheese all over the surface. Cook for a few minutes, until the cheese starts to melt and ooze, then top half the surface with the chorizo slices, peppers, coriander and spring onion. Season with salt and pepper and use a spatula or palette knife to carefully fold the side that has cheese alone over the other filling ingredients. Press gently and cook a few more minutes until everything is warm.

Remove from the heat and use a sharp knife to slice the quesadilla into three. Scatter extra coriander leaves over the top if you wish. You can place the quesadilla under the grill with another layer of grated cheese before slicing if you want a caramelised cheese crust before serving hot (this will definitely fuel you up for the weekend). Squeeze a little lime juice over the quesadilla wedges, if you like, and add Tabasco to taste.

Variations:
– Add a portion of leftover black beans (page 90) to the filling, or some leftover roasted vegetables (page 78), roast sweet potato, leftover chicken or anything else you can raid from the fridge and store-cupboard.
– Add cumin seeds, pimenton, coriander seeds or fennel seeds to the filling.

Savoury cornmeal pancakes with avocado salsa and bacon

Being part-American, I have a nostalgic affection for all things corn – corn muffins, cornbread and grilled sweetcorn laced with lots of butter – so when I was thinking of an alternative to a typical flour-based pancake and spotted a bag of cornmeal in the cupboard I thought, 'Why not?' If you're not a fan of sweetcorn, simply leave it out.

Makes about 5 medium or 8–10 small pancakes

1 tsp vegetable or sunflower oil
3 rashers of bacon

For the avocado salsa
1 small avocado, halved and stoned
2 small tomatoes, roughly chopped
1 fresh red chilli, finely chopped
1 spring onion, thinly sliced
grated zest and juice of ½ lime
1 small bunch of coriander, finely chopped
Tabasco, to taste
salt and black pepper

For the cornmeal pancakes
50g spelt flour or plain flour
50g fine cornmeal
1 tbsp caster sugar or light honey
½ tsp bicarbonate of soda
½ tsp sea salt
150ml buttermilk
50g melted butter, plus extra for frying
1 egg, lightly beaten
100g tinned, drained sweetcorn

Scoop out the avocado flesh and place it in a small-medium bowl. Add the remaining salsa ingredients (except the Tabasco and seasoning). Mix it carefully and let the avocado break up a little but retain a few chunks. Season to taste with Tabasco, salt and pepper. Add more lime juice if you think it needs it, adding more zest too if you like a heady citrus aroma. Set aside.

Preheat the oven to 120°C/gas mark ½.

Sift the flour for the pancakes into a medium bowl and stir in the remaining dry ingredients. Make a well in the middle, add the buttermilk, butter and egg and stir thoroughly. It should be quite velvety and moussy. Stir in the sweetcorn.

Rub a skillet or frying pan with a little butter in an even layer, add a little oil and place over a medium heat. Ladle or spoon 1–2 portions of batter (depending on the size of the pan) into the pan and turn down the heat slightly. Cook the pancake(s) for 2–3 minutes until they form a golden caramel crust underneath, then gently flip the pancake(s) over and cook for a further 2–3 minutes. Place in the warm oven, cook the remaining batter and fry or grill the bacon.

Serve the cornmeal pancakes and bacon with the avocado salsa, and a little extra butter on the pancakes, if you like (delicious, but not essential).

Indian-spiced scrambled eggs (*anda bhurji*)

Spiced scrambled eggs like *anda bhurji* remind me of another brilliant friend: fellow food writer and chef Maunika Gowardhan. As a nod to her I've adapted her super-simple and delicious recipe here. About once a year we go for a big blowout breakfast together, co-opting our other great friend Frances Quinn into a raid of London restaurant Dishoom's exceptional breakfast menu. Bacon naan, a full Bombay-style breakfast, spiced porridge, bottomless refills of chai… and Maunika orders a chocolate pudding for dessert! A woman who feasts at breakfast, and then eats a chocolate dessert at 10:30am, is a woman to be reckoned with. Friendships forged through the occasional act of gluttony really are friendships made to last.

1 tbsp vegetable oil
1 vine tomato or a few smaller
  tomatoes, chopped
1 sprig of coriander, leaves finely
  chopped, plus extra to garnish
1 fresh green chilli, finely chopped
1 shallot, finely chopped
a pinch of ground turmeric
a pinch of chilli powder
a pinch of ground cumin
a pinch of garam masala (optional)
1 tsp butter
2 eggs
sea salt and freshly ground
  black pepper
buttered toast, chapatti, roti roll
  or (for an extra treat) brioche,
  to serve
½ lemon or lime, to serve

Heat the oil in a skillet or small frying pan over a low-medium heat, add the chopped tomato, coriander, green chilli and shallot and cook for about 5 minutes, then add the spices. Season with a little salt and pepper, add the butter and break the eggs into the mixture. Whisk the eggs to combine with the other ingredients, turn down the heat to low and cook for a further 3–5 minutes, stirring gently until the eggs are scrambled.

Serve the scrambled eggs on generously buttered bread of choice, garnish with extra coriander leaves and spritz with lemon or lime juice.

A trio of cheering yoghurts

We all know we need to eat more vegetables on a daily basis, but that can be a challenge. Incorporating them into yoghurt is an easy way to get your 5-a-day – some scientists believe we could even aim for 10-a-day – and they taste much better than those overly-sweet fruit yoghurts you find in the supermarket.

Pale orange: carrot, turmeric and black pepper

500g Greek yoghurt (or plain, for a lighter version)
300g finely grated or puréed carrot
1 tsp ground turmeric
½ tsp freshly ground black pepper
½ tsp ground cinnamon
1 tsp freshly grated ginger

Combine all the ingredients in a bowl. Chill in an airtight container for up to a week.

Green: watercress, parsnip and nutmeg

300g parsnips (2–3 parsnips), quartered or halved lengthways (depending how big they are)
2 tbsp maple syrup
1 tsp vegetable or sunflower oil
½ tsp ground nutmeg
1 bunch of watercress
500g Greek yoghurt (or plain, for a lighter version)
sea salt and freshly ground black pepper

Preheat the oven to 200°C/gas mark 6.

Put the sliced parsnips in a bowl with the maple syrup, oil and nutmeg and rub the parsnips to coat them in the mixture. Place them in a roasting tray or in a baking dish and sprinkle with a pinch of salt. Roast for 20–30 minutes, or until the parsnips are soft and have started caramelising.

Remove from the oven and allow to cool before blitzing in a blender or food processor with the watercress and yoghurt. Taste and season accordingly. Chill in an airtight container for up to a week.

Red/pink: beetroot, horseradish and dill

500g Greek yoghurt (or plain, for a lighter version)
250g cooked beetroot (not pickled)
1 tsp horseradish sauce (or more, if you like it fiery)
1 sprig of dill
a little lemon juice (optional)

Blitz all the ingredients (except the lemon juice) in a blender or mash in a bowl until the beetroot is fully combined with the yoghurt. Taste and season with a little lemon juice if you wish. Chill in an airtight container for up to a week.

Variation: Add some freshly grated orange zest to this if you like.

Sweet
Things

Cherry, almond and dark chocolate tiffin

Sometimes known as the rather prosaic 'Refrigerator Cake', this Tiffin ticks all the boxes: rich, dark chocolate, crunchy biscuits, nutty almonds and the mouth-puckering dried sour cherries.

Some days you just need chocolate. When you don't want cake, or indeed a plain bar of the dark stuff, make this instead.

Cuts into 8–10 slices

150g dark chocolate (I use Green & Black's 70% cocoa solids cooking chocolate), broken into pieces
100g unsalted butter, softened
2 tbsp golden syrup
1 tsp vanilla extract
1 egg
handful of dried sour cherries (about 75g)
handful of toasted flaked almonds
6 digestive biscuits
4 shortbread fingers
a sprinkle of fleur de sel or sea salt (optional)
a sprinkle of cocoa nibs (optional)

Line the base and sides of a 450g loaf tin with cling film (if it doesn't stick, greasing the base with a little oil will act as an adhesive).

Melt the chocolate in a heatproof bowl set over a small saucepan of simmering water, making sure that the bottom of the bowl doesn't touch the water, then remove the bowl from the pan and set it aside to cool slightly.

In a separate bowl, cream the butter with the golden syrup and vanilla for a few minutes until pale. Add the egg and beat rapidly. The mixture may split but it will come together again when you add the chocolate.

Add the melted chocolate, fold everything together and add the cherries and almonds. Roughly crumble the biscuits and shortbread into chunks (if they're too crumbly you won't get that nice crunch when biting into the Tiffin) and fold them in to make a lumpy, chocolatey mess (that's the beauty of Tiffin).

If you'd like a little extra crunch, sprinkle the salt and cocoa nibs on to the bottom of the prepared tin, then spoon the tiffin mixture into the tin and press it down with the back of a spoon or spatula to level out the surface.

Cover with cling film and chill in the fridge for a few hours or overnight. Cut into slices or smaller bites and keep in the fridge for up to a week.

Double chocolate loaf cake

As a lover of dark chocolate I couldn't leave out this delicious loaf cake. If you're shy about baking then this is a doozie – it's quick to make and keeps well so you can treat yourself when the occasion calls for it, or share it with neighbours, friends or colleagues.

I like eating a generous slice of this alongside a cup of green tea or a tall glass of very cold whole milk. Coffee is an obvious partner, too, but if it's been a rough day then there is no shame in pouring a small dram of whisky to sip while you savour the deep chocolate flavour of this cake. Turn a slice into dessert by adding ice cream and some berries, or a little salted caramel sauce.

Cuts into 8–10 slices

175g unsalted butter, softened
175g light brown
  muscovado sugar
1 tsp vanilla extract
¼ tsp fine sea salt
3 eggs, at room temperature
100g self-raising flour, sifted
75g ground almonds
75g cocoa powder
double shot of espresso
¼ tsp bicarbonate of soda
splash of whole milk,
  buttermilk, or slightly diluted
  plain yoghurt (optional)
75g dark chocolate chips
  (70% cocoa solids), or 100g if
  you like it really chocolatey!

Preheat the oven to 170°C/gas mark 3 and line a 900g loaf tin with baking parchment.

Put the butter, sugar, vanilla and salt in a bowl and beat for 5–8 minutes until fluffy and honey-blonde in colour (use an electric whisk or stand mixer if you have one). Add one egg at a time, along with a spoonful of flour (this prevents the mixture from splitting), beating to incorporate each egg into the mixture before adding the next.

Add the remaining flour, almonds, cocoa, espresso and bicarbonate of soda and fold to combine. If the batter is quite dense, add the milk, buttermilk or diluted yoghurt to loosen it. Fold in the chocolate chips.

Spoon the batter into the loaf tin and bake for 40–50 minutes until the top feels firm and a skewer inserted into the middle comes out mostly clean, except for a few crumbs or a smidgeon of melted chocolate chips on it. The baking time will depend on your oven, so check after 35 minutes – it's better to slightly under-bake it than let it sit for too long in the oven.

Place the tin on a wire rack and allow to cool for 15 minutes or so before turning out the cake. It's great warm, but also keeps well for 2–3 days in a sealed container or wrapped in cling film.

Variation: Add toasted chopped walnuts to the mixture when you add the chocolate chips.

Lemon vanilla ice lollies

When we had a rare heatwave, this summertime treat rescued me during recipe testing on days when all I wanted to do was cool off by a pool or dip my feet in the ocean. As a boozy variation, try adding a few tablespoonfuls of vodka or rum to the mixture before freezing.

Makes 6 lollies, or more/less depending on the size of the moulds

**45g fructose (fruit sugar) or
  60g granulated or caster sugar
1 tsp vanilla extract
a pinch of sea salt
100ml water
grated zest of 1 and juice of
  4 medium unwaxed lemons**

Make sure your freezer is at its coldest setting. Have 6 small ice lolly moulds ready.

Put the fructose or sugar in a small saucepan with the vanilla and salt, add the water and bring to a simmer. Let the sugar dissolve completely before removing from the heat. Leave the sugar solution to cool down, then add the lemon juice and zest to the mixture.

Pour the lolly mixture into each lolly mould, insert lolly sticks and freeze for a few hours, or overnight. When you're ready to eat one, remove from the freezer and run the mould under warm water briefly to release the lolly from the mould.

The lollies will keep for a week or two before they start to lose their flavour.

Passionfruit and lime drizzle muffins

Muffins have been a source of delight since childhood, being quick to mix and bake. I'm not so keen on cupcakes (a little too cutesy for my taste, and always laden with way too much sugary frosting) and find these muffins are closer to their British cousin: the fairy cake.

This recipe is an adaptation of Felicity Cloake's phenomenal Lemon Drizzle Cake in the *Guardian*. If you like a classic lemon sponge I really recommend you give her cake a try.

Makes 12 muffins

175g unsalted butter, softened
150g golden caster sugar
1 tsp vanilla extract
¼ tsp fine sea salt
3 eggs, at room temperature
125g self-raising flour, sifted
50g ground almonds
1 tbsp Greek yoghurt
3 ripe passionfruit
grated zest and juice of
  2 unwaxed limes
50g demerara sugar

Preheat the oven to 170°C/gas mark 3 and line a 12-hole mini muffin tin with muffin cases or small squares of baking parchment.

Put the butter, sugar, vanilla and salt in a medium bowl and beat for 5–8 minutes until pale and fluffy (use an electric whisk or stand mixer if you have one). Add one egg at a time, along with a spoonful of flour (this prevents the mixture from splitting), beating to thoroughly incorporate each egg into the mixture before adding the next.

Fold in the remaining flour, almonds and yoghurt with a spatula or metal spoon. Divide the mixture between the muffin cases and bake for 15–20 minutes until the muffins feel firm to the touch and a skewer inserted into one comes out clean.

Remove and let the muffins cool in the tin for a few minutes, then remove from the tin.

Halve the passionfruit and scoop the flesh into a bowl. Add the lime zest and juice, and demerara sugar, and mix to make the drizzle.

Pierce each muffin a few times with a skewer or toothpick while they're still slightly warm (or cool), then spoon the drizzle over each muffin.

Variations: Omit the drizzle and use the sponge mix as a 'base' for other flavours...
– A handful of blueberries or dark chocolate chips.
– Spices such as cardamom, cinnamon and nutmeg.

Peach and strawberry Knickerbocker Glory

Peach Melba, in which raspberries accompany peach, is a classic pairing, but these days we get juicy, ripe peaches from southern Europe earlier in the summer season and they overlap with delicious British strawberries so, naturally, this dish happened. I never tire of fruit-based desserts: a homemade Knickerbocker Glory means you don't have to go out to enjoy a sundae, and is an example of why it's always a good idea to keep a tub of vanilla ice cream in your freezer for impromptu dessert cravings.

handful of ripe strawberries, hulled, plus a few extra to decorate
75ml cold double or whipping cream
1 tsp caster or icing sugar, plus extra for the strawberries
½ tsp vanilla extract
2 scoops of vanilla ice cream
1 ripe peach, peeled, stoned and roughly chopped, or a small portion of Peach Freezer Jam (page 94)
1 shortbread finger, broken up or kept whole
some fructose (fruit sugar), caster sugar or honey, to sweeten the fruit (optional)
1 tsp bright green pistachio nibs (Iranian are best) or toasted flaked almonds (optional)

Crush the strawberries in a bowl with a little sugar and leave them to macerate.

Whisk the cream, teaspoon of sugar and vanilla extract in a bowl for a few minutes until lightly whipped (it should hold its shape).

Place half the ice cream in a tall glass (sundae, cocktail or similar) and top with a few spoonfuls of strawberries, then half the chopped peach. Repeat with the remaining ice cream, peach and strawberries. Spoon over as much cream as you like (keep the rest covered in the fridge for a couple of days to grace coffee, or other desserts).

I like to dunk a shortbread finger into the sundae, but you can also distribute broken biscuit pieces throughout the dessert. Scatter with pistachio nibs or flaked almonds (if using) – the nuts are the final flourish.

Variations:
– Passionfruit makes an excellent addition to a Knickerbocker Glory, especially with a few spoonfuls of good vanilla custard.
– Some like the texture of meringue. I'm not so partial to this, but if you like, add some instead of the shortbread for a little crunch.
– Try cardamom-poached apricots (page 24) instead of peach and strawberries.
– For a boozy dessert, spike the cream with brandy, rum or whisky before you whisk it.

American-style dark and chewy chocolate chip cookies

Early in my career I spent quite a lot of time obsessing over the 'perfect' chocolate chip cookie. Too often the ones you find in supermarkets are overwhelmingly sweet. I wanted the right balance of chewy, with lots of buttery goodness, and a deep brown sugar flavour. This recipe is a hybrid of sorts: I took food scientist Harold McGee's proportions and adapted a cookie recipe from *The Cook's Illustrated Baking Book*. Don't skip the chilling – it's essential to getting the consistency just right.

Honestly, these are so satisfying and you can even turn them into a 'chipwich' – an ice-cream sandwich – should you be so inclined.

Makes 12–15 large cookies or 20–25 smaller cookies

300g plain flour
½ tsp baking powder
¼ tsp bicarbonate of soda
½ tsp fine sea salt
180g butter, melted
200g light brown muscovado sugar
100g golden caster sugar
1 large egg, plus 1 large yolk
1 tsp vanilla extract
150g dark chocolate chips (minimum 70% cocoa solids), or a bar, coarsely chopped into chunks

Line 2 baking sheets with baking parchment and sift the flour, raising agents and salt into a bowl.

Whisk the melted butter in a large bowl with both the sugars, then add the egg, extra yolk and vanilla extract and whisk again. Stir the flour mixture into the wet mixture and beat for a few minutes to really stretch the gluten strands. The cookie dough should be quite solid, almost dry. Work the dark chocolate chips or chunks into the dough, distributing them evenly. Scoop or spoon the cookie dough on to the baking sheets, and chill for a few hours or overnight.

Preheat the oven to 160°C/gas mark 2. Bake the cookies for 15–18 minutes until golden, the sides feel quite firm to the touch but the centre is still quite soft. It's always better to slightly under-bake cookies if you like them chewy.

Cool on a wire rack on their trays, then eat or store in an airtight container for up to a week.

Variations:
– Sprinkle the cookies with sea salt before baking.
– Add chopped almonds, macadamias, pecans or hazelnuts, desiccated coconut or a handful of jumbo oats to the dough.

German fruits of the forest dessert

An understated summertime dish from Germany (*rote grütze*), echoed in Denmark's own *rødgrød med fløde*, this easy dessert makes the most of the abundance of summer berries and fruits you find from May until August across central Europe and the Nordic region. It feels Northern European to me, but you can make it anywhere of course, and given that Britain has such a fantastic array of summer berries it seemed fitting to include it here, not least as a reminder that our German cousins have an underrated cuisine that deserves further exploration.

250g Fruits of the Forest mix
(I like strawberries, cherries, redcurrants, blackberries, gooseberries and blackcurrants), fresh or frozen
150ml water
2 tbsp fructose (fruit sugar) or 3 tbsp granulated sugar
splash of Cherry Heering, cherry brandy or kirschwasser, or sloe gin (optional)
1 tbsp cornflour
crème fraîche, vanilla custard, clotted cream or vanilla ice cream, to serve

Put the fruit mix in a medium saucepan with the water, bring to a simmer over a low-medium heat and cook for 5–10 minutes (if the fruits are frozen they'll take up to 10–15 minutes), or until the fruit starts to dissolve slightly and release lots of colour. Add the fructose or sugar, and alcohol (if using), then cook a further few minutes before tasting for sweetness. Remember this is served cold so you may need to add a little extra sugar, but tread carefully. The joy of *rote grütze* is its tartness.

Mix the cornflour with a tablespoonful of water and whisk it into the fruit mixture, cooking for a final 2–3 minutes, or until it thickens slightly. Remove from the heat and leave to cool.

Chill the berries for a few hours then serve with a dollop of crème fraîche, vanilla custard or a scoop of clotted cream or vanilla ice cream. A little drizzle of kirschwasser on top is a nice touch, but by no means essential to enjoying this dessert.

Variation: In winter, if you have frozen berries lurking in the freezer and wish to make this dish, try adding some warming spices such as cardamom, cinnamon, black pepper, ginger and star anise to the fruits while they're cooking.

Crêpes cherry jubilee

The trick to making good crêpes is to ensure that the consistency of the batter is quite thin so it really spreads around the frying pan or crêpe pan when you ladle it in. This recipe makes 3–4 medium crêpes, but you can easily double or triple it and make a large batch, freezing the extras by separating each cooked crêpe with a strip of baking parchment so you can remove them one at a time from the freezer when needs be. For a savoury crêpe, omit the sugar and vanilla extract.

1 tbsp butter
2 tbsp fructose (fruit sugar) or
  3 tbsp caster sugar
large handful of cherries, halved
  and stoned
lemon juice, to taste (optional)
2 tbsp kirschwasser, cherry
  brandy or Cherry Heering
1–2 scoops of vanilla ice cream

For the crêpes
50g plain flour
1 tsp caster sugar
a pinch of salt
100ml whole milk
25g lightly salted butter,
  melted, plus extra for frying
1 egg, lightly beaten
¼ tsp vanilla extract

To make the crêpe batter, sift the flour into a bowl and add the sugar and salt. Make a well in the middle and whisk in the rest of the ingredients to make a smooth batter. Set it aside for 30 minutes.

When you're ready to cook, place a skillet, frying pan or crêpe pan on the hob for the crêpes and a saucepan on the hob for the cherries. Smear the crêpe pan with a thin layer of butter and put it over a medium heat. Ladle in a little batter and swirl it around. Fry for a few minutes until the edges start to turn golden, then flip it over with a spatula or palette knife. The first crêpe tends to be a dud, but it's still edible. Remove the pancake from the pan and gently wipe the surface of the pan with kitchen paper to remove excess fat. Cook the remaining pancakes.

In the other pan, while cooking the remaining pancakes, melt the butter over a medium-high heat until foaming then add the sugar and cherries. Cook for 5 minutes until the cherries have softened and released juices, then taste, adding a little extra sugar if needed. If they're quite sweet, add lemon juice to cut through the sweetness.

Pour the alcohol into a large metal spoon or ladle and hold it over a flame – it should turn bright blue. Add it to the pan of cherries, swirling it around until the flame dies out.

Spoon the cherry mixture over the crêpes, and serve with ice cream.

Peanut butter buckeyes

Ohio's official tree is the buckeye, and these little treats resemble the nut of the tree. I find the combination of good dark chocolate and a slightly salted peanut butter irresistible, and not only are these buckeyes super-easy to make but the quality of ingredients is better than what you'll find in commercially-produced confectionary. Keep them in the fridge for a week or two, eating one a day and sharing the rest with friends, family and colleagues if you wish…

Makes 12 buckeyes

75g crunchy peanut butter
60g icing sugar
25g butter, melted
¼ tsp vanilla extract
¼ tsp sea salt
50g dark chocolate (70–85% cocoa solids), broken into peices

Put the peanut butter, icing sugar, melted butter, vanilla extract and sea salt in a medium bowl and beat for a minute or two until everything comes together (add a few drops of water to help the mixture bind, if necessary). Using your hands, roll the mixture into 10 balls and place them on a tray or in a box, then transfer to the freezer for 30 minutes to harden the 'buckeyes'.

Melt the chocolate in a heatproof bowl set over a small saucepan of simmering water, making sure that the bottom of the bowl doesn't touch the water. Remove from the heat and, using a skewer or a toothpick, dunk each hardened peanut butter 'buckeye' in the melted chocolate, leaving an 'eye' in the middle (you can, of course, cover the whole 'buckeye' in chocolate if you prefer).

Place each 'buckeye' on a plate or some baking parchment to set, and keep in an airtight container in the fridge for a week or so. These are best eaten cold, straight from the fridge.

Flaming whisky Bananas Foster

Another old-school dessert that is ideal for the solo cook. Bananas have a natural affinity with whisky – especially a whisky with tropical notes (but to be honest their mellow sweetness pairs well with most types). If you don't have whisky to hand, simply substitute with rum or brandy.

1 slightly unripe/green banana
1 tsp butter
2 tsp soft light brown sugar
a pinch of sea salt
a pinch of ground nutmeg or cardamom (optional)
2 tbsp whisky of choice, plus extra to serve (optional)
1–2 scoops of clotted cream or vanilla ice cream
a few crispy maple and cinnamon nuts (opposite), to serve

Have a champagne coupe or cocktail glass at the ready. Slice the banana into about 5 diagonal pieces. Heat the butter in a small skillet or frying pan over a medium heat until foaming, then add the brown sugar and sea salt, stirring a little so they're evenly distributed. Add the banana slices to the pan and fry for about a minute on each side, or until they look golden brown. Remove the pan from the heat and dust the nutmeg or cardamom over the top (if using). Put the whisky in a ladle, and tilt the ladle towards the flame of a gas hob, or light it with a match so it's flaming. Pour the flaming whisky into the pan with the bananas and swirl around until the flame snuffs out.

Scoop as much clotted cream or ice cream as you like into the glass, scatter the hot bananas on top and, if you wish, add another splash of whisky before topping with the crispy nuts. Eat immediately.

Variation: This dish is also excellent with the crêpes from the Crêpes Cherry Jubilee recipe on page 183.

Crispy maple and cinnamon nuts

These are a treat to have on their own, with your morning muesli or porridge, or to add crunch to desserts.

175g mixture of pecans
  and walnuts
25g butter, melted
1 egg white
2–3 tbsp maple syrup or soft
  light brown sugar
½ tsp ground cinnamon
¼ tsp sea salt

Preheat the oven to 180°C/gas mark 4.

Scatter the nuts on a baking tray or cookie sheet and roast for 10 minutes.

Meanwhile, mix the other ingredients together in a bowl large enough to toss the nuts together. Remove the roasted nuts from the oven and turn the heat down to 120°C/gas mark ½.

Toss the nuts in the mixture in the bowl, and scatter all of it back into the same roasting tray (mixture and all). Bake at the lower temperature for 30–40 minutes until crispy.

Remove from the oven and immediately scrape the nuts off the tray (if you leave it to harden it's a nightmare to clean later) and allow to fully cool down on a sheet of baking parchment before storing in an airtight container. Use in the banana recipe opposite, in your porridge or eat as a snack.

Kitchen Kit

I hate to throw cold sarsaparilla on the idea that you can rustle up gourmet meals using just any old coffee mug and a lone spoon, so here's the thing: investing in a few essential kitchen items gives you flexibility when cooking. They don't have to be premium brands: you can find good-value bits of kit online or in the supermarket. I've deliberately steered clear of recommending any fancy chef's kit that you might see on TV, in magazines or on social media. Good cooking happens the world over using not much more than a chopping board, a knife, a bowl, a pan and heat in the form of fire and/or water. If you're new to cooking, here's a list of essential and optional kitchen utensils.

Essentials

knives (1× medium serrated, 1× small chopping knife and 1× larger chef's knife)
*
chopping boards (for bread, fruit, vegetables, meat and fish)
*
Small, medium and large mixing bowls
*
Small, medium and large saucepans
*
Small skillet or frying pan
*
Wok
*
Medium whisk
*
Digital scales
*
2 wooden spoons (for sweet and savoury)
*
Heatproof spatula
*
Good-quality vegetable peeler
*
Ice-cube tray and ice lolly moulds
*
Tubs and freezerproof bags

Pestle and mortar
*
Kitchen scissors (I like Fiskars)
*
A few baking tins (loaf tin, muffin tin and a 22cm round cake tin)
*
Baking sheet
*
3 roasting tins
(small, medium and large)

Handy Extras

Fine Microplane grater
*
Blender for smoothies
*
Stand mixer or electric whisk
*
Handheld blender
*
Food processor with shredder blade
*
Cocktail shaker

Kitchen Staples

Here are the basic ingredients I like to have to hand in my kitchen, and some really useful additions if you have the space.

Cupboard

Basics

sea salt and black pepper
oils: 1 neutral vegetable or olive oil
vinegar: wine or cider vinegar
soy sauce
mustard: dry and/or made
pickles: gherkins, beetroot
noodles (rice/egg) and pasta
rice
dried herbs de Provence and/or
  oregano, bay leaves
spices: chilli flakes/cayenne, cumin,
  coriander seeds, cinnamon, green
  cardamom, garam masala, nutmeg,
  ground turmeric
olives: Spanish manzanilla, Italian
  nocellara, wrinkly black olives
tins: chickpeas, black or other
  beans, plum tomatoes (San Marzano
  DOP are best), fish (such as
  anchovies, mackerel, sardines
  and tuna)
porridge oats
red or other lentils
sourdough crispbread (I love
  Peter's Yard)

Really Useful Additions

harissa paste (Belazu is great)
Japanese soba buckwheat noodles
Japanese nori (dried seaweed)
dried kombu and/or wakame (for
  making vegetarian stock)
oils: toasted sesame, walnut, argan,
  an extra-virgin olive oil for salads/
  dressing
vinegars: balsamic, sherry, fruit vinegars
mirin
nuts: almonds, walnuts, pecans,
  pistachio and pine nuts
salad cream and mayonnaise
pomegranate molasses
Worcestershire sauce
Tabasco
horseradish sauce
Thai fish sauce
ponzu
tahini
peanut butter and/or almond butter
dried mushrooms (porcini, shiitake
  and/or a wild mushroom mix)
capers
preserved lemons
couscous (barley or regular)
jarred jalapeños
firm and/or silken tofu

tins: sweetcorn, pumpkin purée,
  artichoke hearts
bulgur wheat
semolina
sesame seeds
pimenton dulce/picante
fennel seeds
fine or rough cornmeal

Sweet Things and Baking

Basics

flours: plain, wholemeal, strong
  white, cornflour
sugars: golden caster, soft light brown
  sugar, icing sugar, demerara sugar
golden syrup
runny honey
bicarbonate of soda
baking powder
dried fruits: apricots, figs, prunes,
  dates
unsweetened cocoa powder
  (Green & Black's is good)
dark chocolate (70–85%
  cocoa solids)
vanilla extract (not essence)

Really Useful Additions

flours: sprouted spelt, rice flour
fruit sugar
black treacle
maple syrup
set honey and acacia honey
sour cherries
cocoa nibs
sour cherries
packets of your favourite biscuits:
  all-butter shortbread, digestives
  and ginger nuts (which can all lift
  a simple, impromptu dessert)

Bottles

(for cooking and for the cook)

vermouth
fino or manzanilla sherry
brandy and/or whisky of choice
porter or stout
red and white wine
cherry brandy

My Favourite Fresh Ingredients

Fridge

Basics

plain, unsweetened, full-fat yoghurt
  and/or thick Greek yoghurt
butter
cheese: blue, Parmesan, halloumi,
  Cheddar, a good melter (Gruyere,
  Comte, Jarlsberg, etc.), ricotta
medium free-range eggs (can also be
  kept at room temperature)
milk
bacon, pancetta, jamon or chorizo

Really Useful Additions

miso: red or brown
Korean kimchi
seafood: hot-smoked salmon/trout,
  smoked salmon, mackerel, herrings
smoked chicken, pastrami or turkey

Freezer

Basics

ice!
vegetables: soffritto mix, broad
  beans, peas, spinach
bread, sliced
berries
fish fingers

peeled, chopped bananas for
  smoothies and shakes
vanilla ice cream for quick desserts

Really Useful Additions

bag of fruits de mer
freshly chopped herbs in oil (rosemary,
  thyme and lemongrass keep well)
frozen seasonal fruit: blood orange
  slices for drinks, chopped rhubarb
  (for impromptu compote or crumble)
  and watermelon
freezer jam (page 94)
batches of Bolognese Ragù Sauce
  (page 78), Basic Tomato Sauce
  (page 103), Beef, Porter and Barley
  Stew (page 96) and stock (see Chicken
  Stock, opposite) (keep concentrated
  stock in ice-cube trays)
lemon sorbet
milk, butter and cheese

Countertop

a few unwaxed lemons
garlic
banana shallots and/or red onions
green and/or red chillies
seasonal fruit
small pots of herbs

Chicken Stock

Strip the carcass from the roast bird on page 97 and place
the bones, gristly bits and a little of the skin in a saucepan.
Add aromatics such as black peppercorns, garlic, parsley stems,
fennel bulbs or fronds (and seeds), celery, carrots and onions,
cover with about double the amount of water and bring to a
simmer. Keep the heat on low-medium (you don't want the
chicken bones to boil) and let it simmer gently for a few hours.
Strain to remove all the bones, gristly bits and aromatics then
simmer the strained stock over a medium heat until reduced
by half (if you want a really concentrated flavour reduce it to
a quarter of its volume). Let it cool, then pour it into an ice-cube
freezer tray or two for future use. Use the stock as a base for
chicken soup, adding leftover roast chicken, noodles, vegetables
and herbs for an instant 'Jewish Penicillin'.

Suppliers

Although major UK supermarkets have an impressive
array of ingredients from around the world, sometimes
I want to cook with ingredients that aren't so widely
available. These are reliable online retailers.

– Sous Chef (www.souschef.co.uk)
Fantastic for any ingredients that might be a little harder
to source at your local supermarket

– The Japan Centre (www.japancentre.com)
Terrific for noodles, sauces, teas and, well, all things Japanese!

– www.amazon.co.uk
Has a good selection of cooking ingredients, especially
in larger sizes if you're thinking of buying in bulk

– The Scandi Kitchen (www.scandikitchen.co.uk)
Always a reliable source of Scandinavian ingredients

– Seasoned Pioneers (www.seasonedpioneers.com)
Does a really nifty line of seasonings and spices

– Andreas Veg (www.andreasveg.co.uk)
While I was recipe testing, I relied on Andreas Georghiou
for fresh produce deliveries

Index

Signe Johansen is a Norwegian–American cook and author of *How to Hygge* and *Spirited: The Joy of Drinks* (Bluebird), *Scandilicious* and *Scandilicious Baking* (Saltyard Books), and *Peter's Yard: Smörgåsbord* (Kyle Books). A longtime whisky enthusiast, she is the co-founder of 'Spirited Women', a project to get more women into whisky and other spirits. After graduating with a bachelor's degree in archaeology and anthropology from the University of Cambridge, she trained at Leiths School of Food and Wine in London, worked in several of the UK's top restaurants and went on to do her masters in the anthropology of food at SOAS Food Studies Centre at the University of London. She has appeared on *Kirstie's Handmade Christmas*, *What's Cooking* and *Sunday Brunch*. She lives in Bloomsbury, London.

Acknowledgements

This book may have been penned by a solo cook but I have a whole team of talented people to thank for sprinkling their magic into producing this fine object you're holding right now…

Thank you to my agent Sarah Williams at the Sophie Hicks Agency, a gal with the best taste in places to drink wine while we talk through ideas.

To the Bluebird team at Pan Macmillan, my thanks to the brilliant Carole Tonkinson, Martha Burley, Hockley Raven Spare, Jessica Farrugia, Jodie Mullish and Ami Smithson for all your hard work, and constant encouragement. To Laura Nickoll for being such a patient copy editor and project manager of this book.

To the always-cheerful *Solo* Photographic Team: Thank you Patricia Niven, Jess Griffiths, Rosie Reynolds, Esther Clark and Linda Berlin. Thank you also to Nadira V Persaud and Jerry Khan for making me look way more put-together at the shoot than my usual scruffy self. I'd also like to extend my thanks to the White Company and Jigsaw for supplying clothing for the portrait shoot.

Many thanks to the friends and colleagues who kindly shared their thoughts on cooking solo with me: Mark Newton, Simon Majumdar, Melissa Cole, Silvia Dee, Jamie Schler, Andrew Wiggins, Catherine Phipps, Simon Radford, Louise Marston, Charles Justin Sheng, Johanna Kindvall, Eleanor Perkin-Brown, Niamh Shields, Sarah Pettegree, Tracey Ruck, Ailbhe Phelan, Jason B. Standing, Tricia Mundy, Richard Gray, Elena Sidorochkina, Jane Baxter, Elissa McGee, Claire Nelson, Hannah McCarthy, Tom Harrow, Rosie Lovell, Kim Katharina, John Shields, Lynne Clark, Zoe Aldam, Richard Bertinet, Lynda Reid, and also to Sue Quinn for reminding me of a great Nigel Slater quote about cooking for yourself being an act of self-respect. Amen to that. Thank you as always to the most spirited of women, Fiona Beckett and Diana Henry, for being sources of constant inspiration.

Finally, I owe a lifetime's debt of gratitude to my parents, Jane and Jan, and to Mungo Wenban-Smith, for accompanying me on long walks by the sea or through the woods when I needed to clear my head, and for their continual love and support.

First published 2018 by Bluebird
an imprint of Pan Macmillan
The Smithson, 6 Briset Street, London EC1M 5NR
EU *representative*: Macmillan Publishers Ireland Limited,
Mallard Lodge, Lansdowne Village, Dublin 4

Associated companies throughout the world
www.panmacmillan.com

This paperback edition first published 2021

ISBN 978-1-5290-6494-0

9 8 7 6 5 4 3 2 1
A CIP catalogue record for this book is available from the British Library
Printed and bound in China

Publisher *Carole Tonkinson*
Desk Editor *Isabel Hewitt*
Project Editor *Katy Denny*
Managing Editor *Martha Burley*
Senior Production Controller *Sarah Badhan*
Design *Ami Smithson*
Prop Styling *Linda Berlin*
Food Styling *Rosie Reynolds*

Visit **www.panmacmillan.com** to read more about all our books and to buy
them. You will also find features, author interviews and news of any author
events, and you can sign up for e-newsletters so that you're always first to
hear about our new releases.